the Christ-CENTERED HEART

the Christ-CENTERED HEART

peaceful living
in difficult times

RICK MATHIS, Ph.D.

LIGUORI/TRIUMPH
LIGUORI, MISSOURI

Published by Liguori/Triumph
An Imprint of Liguori Publications
Liguori, Missouri

Library of Congress Cataloging-in-Publication Data

    The Christ-centered heart : peaceful living in difficult times /
Rick Mathis, Ph.D. — 1st ed.
      p. cm.
    ISBN 0-7648-0387-5
    1. Love—Religious aspects—Christianity. 2. Spiritual Life.
I. Title.
BV4639.M3345   1999
248.4—dc21   98-47860

Contents

v

Introduction

Just then a lawyer stood up to test Jesus. "Teacher,"
he said, "what must I do to inherit eternal life?"
He said to him, "What is written in the law? What
do you read there?" He answered, "You shall love
the Lord your God with all your heart, and with
all your soul, and with all your strength, and with
all your mind; and your neighbor as yourself." And
he said to him, "You have given the right answer;
do this, and you will live."

Luke 10:25–28

Recently, I heard of an old acquaintance who had
gone through a painful divorce. He suspected that
his wife was having an affair and set up elabo-
rate schemes to catch her. As it turns out, he was abso-
lutely right. Not content to divorce her and have done
with it, however, he now spends his time brooding over
what happened, reliving the painful events again and
again. Bitter and angry, he has lost a great deal of weight
and is hardly recognizable to those who know him. Even
though some time has passed since the divorce, he is
unable to get on with his life. He spends most of his time

devising ways of making his former wife's life miserable. When he is not doing that, he tries to see how many of his own affairs he can have. He is the embodiment of vengeance and hate.

Such are the real situations of life. If life were easy, if people never let us down, if no one ever made us jealous or angry, then it would be easy for us to love. The truth is that we are all bound to suffer serious setbacks and betrayals in our lives. You need only look at the divorce statistics to see that such serious life events happen to a large segment of the population. This is to say nothing of such difficulties as career setbacks and drug and alcohol problems. Life is filled with sorrow.

But is it really? To say that life is comprised of sorrow says nothing of the fact that our lives are really made up of two components—what happens to us, and how we react to what happens to us. There is much that has been made of this simple fact over the years. There are quotations saying that life is what we make of it, and books written about how we choose our reactions to the events that happen to us. I don't think it's that simple, however. I'm not sure that we can gain total control of our psyches, turning our reactions on and off as if we were robots pushing buttons to determine our emotions at any given time. Instead, we must look at our individual selves and understand that we are prone to react a certain way to certain situations, and that one person's reactions to events will differ from those of another. This deeper understanding gives us a better chance of changing our reactions to the world.

Let's return to my jealous friend. I can understand and sympathize with him to an extent because I myself am prone to jealousy (my wife can attest to this). There are people out there who would have even a harder time than my friend and who might become suicidal or violent as a result of the same set of events. Conversely, there are people who are hardly jealous at all, who would be able to get on with their lives without much of a disruption.

This brings us to the theme of this book. As I see it, the most appropriate response to all situations is love. The trick is to be able to love when life gets hard or when something comes along that pushes your unique set of buttons. How do you get to love in facing the sting of infidelity, for example, when your marriage is the most important thing in your life? Similarly, how do you recover when a trusted friend lets you down, when that friendship was what carried you through previous difficulties?

These are tough issues. It would be flip to suggest that we can get through them with just a change in our thought processes. We are much more complex than that. The challenge remains, though, to move past hatred and anger to love. Beyond this is the challenge of exhibiting love throughout all of life, through the highs, the middles, and the lows.

The argument of this book is that our ability to get to love is enhanced by centering our lives upon Christ. A Christ-centered life changes our perspective, turning us as much as possible from a life built around our own needs to one built around the love of God and the love of others. This, as we see from the quotation at the beginning of this introduction, is the path to eternal life.

One means of searching into how we love is to focus on the heart. The heart is typically seen as the seat of emotion. In many respects, it is the center of our emotional self. What does this mean? Of course, we must be speaking metaphorically, for we can't really dissect the heart to find where our "self" comes from. But is this really a total metaphor? After all, it is the heart, according to physicians, that is most impacted by strong emotions. A growing body of literature is even linking emotional difficulties (i.e., anger, stress, and fear) with heart disease. Even the symptoms of stress (increased heart rate, rapid breathing, constriction of the arteries leading to the heart) indicate a connection between the emotions and the cardiovascular system. The same can be said of a peaceful state (slower pulse, deeper breathing, less constriction).

More important, I believe that in some ways the heart gauges our internal experience. In a description that is somewhere between metaphor and reality, we *feel* with our hearts. That is, we experience love, joy, and peace, just as we experience hatred, anger, and disquiet, from our hearts.

This idea provides a powerful means of understanding and experiencing a Christ-centered life. Such a life will be one in which the heart, in that concrete *and* metaphorical way, is filled with the love of Christ. We will know that our hearts are filled with this love when they are changed to the extent that we manifest greater degrees of love, joy, and peace. The commandments to love God and love our neighbor, intricately linked as they are, will become our life's blood.

The path traveled is from inside to out. We begin with the realization that the way we react to situations, and to life in general, comes from within us. If we are ever to love God and our neighbor, we must work with ourselves and understand ourselves better. Once we do, we will be able to interact with the world in a more loving way and to reap the great joys of such an interaction.

Chapter 1 establishes the importance of love in the Bible and how the view of love found there is in many ways different from our practice of it. This chapter ends with a look at how our lives would be if we took the biblical view seriously. In essence, this chapter presents something of the idea behind a Christ-centered heart. Chapter 2 examines some common problems that get in the way of love. These emotions come up like storms within us, tossing us about on an angry sea. Chapter 3 looks at the possibility of calming these waters, both from a psychological and a spiritual perspective. Such a calming influence is important to leading a Christ-centered life. Chapter 4 explores further the practical application of spiritual ideas to everyday life. Chapters 5, 6, and 7 deepen this approach by tracking a movement from inside to out, exploring what it means to lead a Christ-centered life and how this changes the heart. Chapter 8 looks specifically at prayer as a unique feature of a centered heart, while chapter 9 looks at wisdom as a feature of such a heart. Chapter 10 concludes with some final thoughts on the reasons for and the methods to a Christ-centered heart. Each chapter ends with some techniques and exercises designed to assist you on your journey to a Christ-centered heart and life.

The hope in all of this is that together we will expand the experience of love in our lives, as pertains to loving both God and our neighbors. This "expansion" is joyous, but it is not always easy. Many times our first reaction to life's events is hate, and many aspects of our world reinforce this reaction. Elements of life, and some of the people around us, will tell us that our hate is justified, and that to act otherwise is cowardly and wrong. There is, however, a more "excellent way," to quote Saint Paul on love (1 Corinthians 12:31). Changing our hearts grants the possibility of expanding our experience of love. This expansion will not lead you down the path of emptiness and false pride that may characterize your current journey. It is a movement into the kingdom of God and all the joys associated with that kingdom.

ONE

Love Is Kind

L ove is cruel. Consider the times when someone you love has let you down. Perhaps a close relative, who should love you by virtue of your family connection, took advantage of you. Or perhaps a close friend in whom you confided betrayed a trust. Maybe someone you dearly loved slighted you with cutting words in front of others and then refused to discuss it when you confronted him or her in private.

Even closer to home, consider the times when *you* have been unkind. Have you ever done something that, if it came to the light of day, would cause pain to someone you love? Or have you engaged in slanderous talk behind a coworker's back? Maybe you have been less than trusting of your significant other, turning to jealousy or anger when you should have been understanding. Perhaps you are divorced and still unable to forgive your former spouse, even to the point of using your children to exact revenge.

These kinds of things happen all the time. How can

1

one say, then, that love is kind? That's exactly what the Bible says in the famous thirteenth chapter of 1 Corinthians. Even though this chapter is often quoted, it is worthwhile repeating what it says here because it is so starkly different from what we experience in daily life. Beginning with the fourth verse, Saint Paul says:

> Love is patient; love is kind; love is not envious or boastful or arrogant or rude. It does not insist on its own way; it is not irritable or resentful; it does not rejoice in wrongdoing, but rejoices in the truth. It bears all things, believes all things, hopes all things, endures all things. Love never ends (13:4–8).

Now these are an unusual set of propositions. "Love is patient and kind." Think of parents with their children. At the end of a long, hard day, parents are often ready to jump all over their children for the slightest offense. "Love is not envious or boastful." Do we always feel so happy when our friends, whom we love, are wildly successful? Do we never brag about our own or our children's accomplishments? "Love is not irritable or resentful." I've seen a lot of irritability between people who supposedly love one aother. And not resentful? I recently saw a large handwritten sign on the back windshield of a passing car that said something to the effect of "John _____ is a Deadbeat Dad." Here, I thought, are two people who once loved each other and even had children whom they loved. Now one of them is rejecting his financial responsibility to support and protect his children, and the other is initiating an advertising campaign about it. So much for not being resentful.

So how can Saint Paul say what he does about love? Isn't love liable to produce envy and resentment? Everyone is bound to let us down in life, and it is particularly painful when it's someone we love. Yet that will happen often enough.

Obviously, Saint Paul is talking about something much different from the kind of love we are prone to experience. These verses from 1 Corinthians are describing an ideal or perfect view of love. This ideal is not incomprehensible. Love, in fact, ought to be patient and kind. It ought to be supportive of the beloved to the extent that the lover is not easily angered and is always ready to wipe the slate clean. We recognize these "oughts." Perhaps that is one reason why we are so hurt when someone we love lets us down. They aren't acting the way they are supposed to. We expect them to be more understanding and more supportive. We expect them to act in a loving way rather than falling short of the ideal.

Heaven forbid, though, that anyone should apply this standard to us!

We do have a living example of this type of ideal love. This, as we are taught from childhood, is the way God loves us. God does not delight in our evil actions but rejoices in our good ones. God is patient with us and so protective of us that God was willing to send Jesus to die for our sins. And like the father in the parable who runs to greet his prodigal son, God is always ready to take us back, regardless of our depravity. God is always ready not only to forgive us but to celebrate our return. This is a love that never fails.

So we experience perfect love in our relationship with the Divine Presence. Does this model of love have any significance for us in our relations with one another? We don't have to look far to see that it does. Saint Paul is writing not so much to describe God's love of us but to emphasize the importance of love and the need to share this kind of love. In the opening verses of chapter 13 he talks about the gifts that people have, whether they be prophesying or knowledge or faith. These gifts, however, mean nothing if we do not love.

The need to love one another is stressed elsewhere in the Bible. We are called upon to love our neighbors as ourselves and to be very deliberate about putting this love into practice. When asked which are the greatest commandments—the commandments leading to eternal life—Jesus responds with "loving God" and "loving our neighbors." When asked who are our neighbors, Jesus tells the story of the Good Samaritan (Luke 10:25–37). This story indicates not only the importance of practicing love by helping those we may be inclined to pass by but also the fact that there are no social limitations on those who can act like a neighbor and thereby live the eternal life. The man who helped the person in distress was, of course, among the hated tribe of Samaria.

So how do we begin to practice this love of our neighbor, this love that never fails? As I write this, I think about my own tendencies toward imperfect love. Many years ago I sat in a corporate training course designed to assess a person's personality type. I was impressed by how accurately I was captured by the test. What disturbed me, though, was one particular trait my type has. I keep a running tally of the wrongs committed against me by the people in my life. I thought about arguments that I'd gotten into with my wife. True to my type, I am prone to come out with a verbal list of all the ways I feel she has wronged me, a meticulous list that stretches over a number of years. I tend to do the same thing with other people in my life, reflecting in moments of anger on how they have let me down and thinking in detail about every instance.

What are we to do when confronted with this notion of perfect love? The rest of this book will be a response to this question. For now, let's start with a three-step process to get us beyond the obvious shortcomings we exhibit in our own love lives. Then we will talk a little more about how to drive this three-step process even deeper into our hearts.

The first step leading to a more perfect love is to *acknowledge the Corinthian vision as superior to the way we currently are in our relationships*. This is not so easy as it sounds. When we fall short of ideal love, we usually feel that we are justified in doing so. We have a right to be angry or jealous, for example, given whatever circumstance we may be facing. Aren't we just reacting the way a "reasonable" person would? Isn't our reaction rational and justified?

Is it really? To say this with certainty, we must argue for our being (as individuals) the ultimate rational person. We must assume a "godlike" stature and claim to be free of any individual biases. This, we know, is absurd.

It's helpful to look at how good we feel when we have decided to react in a way other than that described in 1 Corinthians. How good does anger feel? How pleasurable is jealousy? How enjoyable is it to attempt to control others when such control is usually impossible and many times succeeds only in pushing people away? This is not to say that there are no instances when such emotions as anger are justified (think of Jesus' throwing the moneychangers out of the Temple). Being human, however, we are prone to possess negative emotions much more frequently, and exhibit them much more quickly, than is necessary. When we are overcome by these emotions, we are nowhere near happy. Nor are we positive and blissful influences on those around us.

Practicing patience and kindness, and being slow to anger, simply is a more appropriate response to our neighbors. It also *feels* better in a way that can't quite be documented as much as experienced, though a recent school of psychology called the Psychology of Mind does provide some corroboration. As described by leading proponent Richard Carlson, this approach maintains that what a person focuses on determines his or her inner state. If a person chooses to dwell on negative, angry thoughts, then he or she will embody all of the manifestations of such thoughts (anger, depression, and so on). A person who is slow to anger is going to have a much easier time keeping a healthy and happy outlook on life.

"Your experience of life," Carlson argues, "is directly related to where you choose to focus your attention. If you focus on your thoughts of problems, your experience of life will consist of mainly problems. As you learn to move your focus of attention away from the problems and wrongs of the world and your life, you will find yourself noticing more beauty and kindness."[1] This is perfectly in tune with the 1 Corinthians view of love.

After accepting the Corinthian view of love as the best, the next step is to *identify your strengths and weaknesses against it.* What have people told you are your strong points with respect to the Corinthian characteristics? Are you particularly patient? Are you fairly content and not envious of others? What about your weaknesses? Perhaps you are a bit of a narcissist and have such difficulty getting past your own boasting and posturing that you fail even to pay attention to the people around you. Perhaps you delight in the failures and mistakes of others and can't wait to criticize them behind their backs. Let's face it, we all have these negative tendencies. It's important, though, to know our own particular weaknesses, as well as our strengths.

You might go so far as to list all of the characteristics in chapter 13 of 1 Corinthians and write a brief summary of where you are with respect to each. How are you in the kindness category? What would you need to do to improve here? How are you with respect to boasting? Could you use a little more humility in your life? If you dare, you might share this list with others to see if the way you view yourself matches the way they see you.

Step 3 is to *find ways of putting the Corinthian view into practice.* This is not going to be easy because it requires you to act differently from the way you have in the past. This step involves several practices. One is to look at your strengths as identified in step 2 and find ways of expanding them into other areas of your life. These are your gifts, and you can bring a lot of peace and joy to others by using them.

You also need to look at your shortcomings, of course. These are the areas where God intends for you to do some work. The best way to proceed is to look prayerfully at these areas and ask God to help you find ways of improving your ability to love. Prayer is, in fact, the most important aid in learning how to love in the Corinthian way. Prayer allows you to open yourself honestly to God and enables you to find guidance from God in terms of what you need to do to love better.

A final part of step 3 is to undertake an ongoing assessment of where you are. You need to realize that you will never match the perfection outlined in the letter to the Corinthians. Being human, you will always fall short in some area. The idea, though, is to be open to a process of sanctification, working toward exhibiting a greater degree of love in your life.

Being open to grace means also that we look for a means of driving the process of being a better lover deeper into our hearts. The truth is that we can't do this on our own. We are too prone to draw from our individual egotistical interests in reacting to others. We need to find a means for getting past ourselves.

One of the best ways of doing this is to live within the presence of God on a moment-to-moment basis. Most of the time, we focus on ourselves and whatever situation is confronting us. Missing is a focus upon God. Believe it or not, you can continually focus upon the presence of God no matter where you find yourself. It merely involves keeping God's presence in your heart while interacting with others or doing your daily tasks. The result of this practice is a greater experience in the participation and the sharing of love. This is part and parcel of Jesus' emphasis upon loving God and loving your neighbor.

A disarmingly simple spiritual classic written by a French monk of the seventeenth century captures this realization well. Brother Lawrence of the Resurrection's *The Practice of the Presence of God* talks of the joys and difficulties involved in communing with God throughout all of life's experiences. His simple message is that the way to holiness is through doing *all* things with God intimately present before us. Since God is love, we will naturally experience greater love in doing this. We will also exhibit a greater degree of love in our interactions with others. As Henri J. M. Nouwen writes in a foreword to one translation of this classic, "When we are concerned with God and God alone then we discover that the God of our prayer is the God of our neighbor. Therefore: The closer we come to God, the closer we come to each other."[2]

The Abbé de Beaufort, who wrote brief summaries of his four personal conversations with Brother Lawrence, captured the spirit of Brother Lawrence's outlook. Abbé de Beaufort remembered Brother Lawrence as saying that "after having given much thought," he had concluded that the shortest path to God "was by a continual exercise of love, while doing all things for the love of God."[3] This love involves acting with God present. It is not the case, as one might think, of setting aside large portions of the day for constant prayer, as if these are the only times when God is to be experienced. Instead, de Beaufort recalled Brother Lawrence's saying that it was a great delusion to think that "time set aside for prayer should be different from other times, that we were obliged equally to be united to God by work in the time assigned to work as by prayer during prayer time."[4]

Brother Lawrence himself identified the following six practices as necessary to attain the spiritual life:

1. Become accustomed to God and learn to be with God at all times.
2. Talk intimately with God, carrying on "little conversations" with God.
3. Carry out all of our actions with care and wisdom, working "peacefully, tranquilly, and lovingly with God."
4. Make sure we stop during all our activities to adore God "from the bottom of our hearts."
5. Recognize that God is truly in our hearts at all times.
6. Ascertain the virtues that we lack and the sins we most frequently fall into and ask "lovingly for the help of [God's] grace."[5]

These practices represent, I think, our best means of allowing God to change our hearts. Unless we center our hearts upon God through Christ, we remain slaves to our personal needs and passions. Recognizing the presence of God frees us from this slavery. By living within this presence, "the soul comes to know God in such a way that it passes almost all of its life in making continual acts of love, adoration, contrition, trust, actions of grace, offering, petition, and of all the most excellent virtues; and sometimes it even becomes one endless act because the soul is always engaged in staying in this divine presence."[6] This, I believe, is another way of affirming and living within the Corinthian vision of love.

Can we embody a love that never fails? This, of course, is not going to be easy. A friend told me recently of a person at his company whom everyone tries to avoid. Jane appears to be pleasant enough at first, but soon she really gets on your nerves. She begins by doing what she can to be your friend. She goes too far, in fact. She begs you to eat lunch with her, have a drink with her after work, and let her spend time with your family. She is almost comical in her pursuits. The problem is, once a "victim" relents and goes somewhere with her, she only steps up her efforts. If she eats lunch with you once, she wants to do it all the time. If she has dinner with you at a restaurant, she then tries to wrangle an invitation to your house. Beyond this, Jane has the annoying habit of lying about facts, figures, and events in order to "prove" that whatever opinion she has is correct. As a result, her associates face an intrusive person who is constantly misrepresenting the truth and who is never able to be "wrong." In no time at all, Jane becomes too much to handle, and practically everyone working in her area avoids her at all costs.

How will practicing the presence of God, and trying to live within the Corinthian vision, help a person deal with someone such as Jane? We've probably all known someone like this at one time or another. Such people try the most patient and kind types of love. Still, taking Brother Lawrence's view can allow us to interact with someone like Jane without hating him or her. It can allow us to experience God within and to use that experience to continue to interact with Jane in a loving way. The presence of God can also allow us to discern the difficulties that are going to get in the way of the interaction and to do something about them. We might tell Jane what our limits are and point out, when necessary, the fallacies of her "facts" without being hateful or even ill-mannered. So the practice of the presence of God will help us deal with even this most difficult of situations in a way that expands the experience of love within ourselves and others. It can keep us from discounting or dismissing someone totally—which we in our society are all too ready to do.

Love often fails, but the ideal of love continues. It is, in fact, something we experience in our relationship with God. We can allow God to become so much a part of our lives that we come to a more intimate understanding of perfect love and begin to exhibit this love toward others. In the next chapter we will discuss in more detail the human tendencies that prevent us from showing more love in our relationships with God and with others. Before doing this, however, let's end this chapter with the first of our practical exercises on our journey toward a Christ-centered life.

The Journey: A Beginning

If Saint Paul is right, then a Christ-centered life is one in which love is paramount. We also see this in 1 John, which says quite simply that "God is love" (1 John 4:16). Saint John also says, "This is his commandment, that we should believe in the name of his Son Jesus Christ and love one another, just as he has commanded us. All who obey his commandments abide in him, and he abides in them. And by this we know that he abides in us, by the Spirit that he has given us" (1 John 3:23–24). Placing Christ at the center of your life—which is to live in him—will bring about a sense of love. This comes from the Holy Spirit, which Christ has given us.

As you begin your journey toward a Christ-centered life, try this simple exercise. Spend five minutes each morning in centering upon Christ, actually picturing him in your heart. Feel the sense of joy and love that this brings about. And that's it. Just experience that pure sense of love, independent from everything else, for the first few minutes of each day.

TWO

The Sea of the Self

Many times our emotional life seems as if it is a stormy sea of discord. We are tossed about by our emotions, riding on waves of distress. Our anger with someone may consume us, nearly drowning us in emotion. Or we may be so filled with our own ambition that we have room for little else in our lives. We look for some peaceful shore but can't seem to find it. We feel doomed to be the way we are, to sail a course over which we have no control.

This is what it is like to live for too long outside of the experience of God's love. We may even feel like Jesus' disciples when they were in the middle of a lake during a storm. Saint Luke tells it this way:

> One day he got into a boat with his disciples, and he said to them, "Let us go across to the other side of the lake." So they put out, and while they were sailing he fell asleep. A windstorm swept down on the lake, and the boat was filling with water, and they were in danger. They went to him and woke him

14

up, shouting, "Master, Master, we are perishing!"
And he woke up and rebuked the wind and the
raging waves; they ceased, and there was a calm.
He said to them, "Where is your faith?" They were
afraid and amazed, and said to one another, "Who
then is this, that he commands even the winds and
the water, and they obey him?" (Luke 8:22–25).

Many times when we are sailing along smoothly we
hit an unexpected storm. Someone criticizes us and
wounds us deeply, or some bad event takes place. We
are immediately thrown into a panic. We wonder where
our Savior is. If we think about him at all, we may feel
that he has fallen asleep. The problem is, however, that
it is we who have failed to awaken him in our hearts. We
must learn how to do this to brave life's worst storms.
It's not a difficult process. We merely need to call on him
and learn to live with him at our center. There we will
find the calmness that we need.

Why do we forget to do the simple thing of asking for
Christ's help? Mainly because we get caught up in the
storm. The storm, remember, is within us. It is our passions and our emotions. It's difficult to pull back from
these and open ourselves to Christ. It just seems as if we
are too intimately caught up in what is happening within
us and around us.

How do we get a grip? One way is to understand the
actions that are bound to set us adrift. Those listed in
Saint Paul's letter to the Galatians are good candidates
for consideration. These are "fornication, impurity, li-
centiousness, idolatry, sorcery, enmities, strife, jealousy,

anger, quarrels, dissensions, factions, envy, drunkenness, carousing, and things like these" (5:19–21). Here we will look at a few of them: those associated with sexual immorality, hatred and anger, jealousy, rage, envy, and destructive ambition. Any one of these can cause our lives to go careening off course, but we will go on to look at the other side: that is, how to weather life's storms through a Christ-centered focus that brings self-control.

Sexual Immorality

I once heard a minister say what in our society is the unthinkable. It was a sermon that he delivered on a Sunday that happened to fall on Valentine's Day. The topic, appropriately enough, was romantic love.

"Sex outside of marriage," he said, "is a mistake."

He did not say this in a condemning way, but just as a matter of fact based upon the Bible's wisdom.

No one, of course, rose to disagree with him. Still, I thought about all the people whom I know who in one way or another make this "mistake." It's not that these people don't consider themselves to be Christians. Many attend church and would certainly consider themselves to be good followers of Christ. It is simply true that we no longer determine whether someone is a Christian by their sexual behavior. The lines have become too blurred.

Sexuality has taken such a central place in our society that the very notion of sexual immorality seems to be dropping out of fashion. Simply having sex with someone that one has dated a few times is not considered immoral. Even adultery doesn't carry the stigma that it once did. Sex, it seems, has become so vitally important to our view of human nature that to suggest that an unmarried person live without it is almost the same as saying that they live without sleeping or eating. And to suggest that any restraints be put on people, married or unmarried, is becoming passé.

This is why the whole issue of sexual immorality is so difficult to address in today's society. Still, what Saint Paul says about sexual immorality as a mark of a sinful nature is telling even to us. The problem with sexual license is that it takes our focus off of spiritual matters. Someone can't be thinking too much about God when in the throes of an extramarital affair. Sexual immorality is likely to bring about other extremely undesirable passions too. Jealousy and hatred, which we will soon discuss, often result from adultery. These emotions frequently take a violent turn. Even in the relatively small community where I live hardly a day passes when someone doesn't kill or injure another person as a result of jealousy or adultery. This is to say nothing of the heartache of divorce, which is especially acute when it involves families with children.

With a projected two-thirds of marriages ending in divorce, however, it no longer makes sense from a practical standpoint to rail against it. I have known many fine people who, for one reason or another, decided to end their marriages. For purposes of this discussion, we need to recognize any role that sexual immorality may have had in such an event and that it does make sense to recommit to sexual morality, to focus more strongly on God and control anger and jealousy. Whatever your current situation, now is the time to commit to at least a monogamous relationship, so that sexuality can take its proper place in your life.

While we will talk more about this later, the following principles are helpful in establishing a sexual morality even in these uncertain times:

1. *See your sexuality as part of your spirituality.* This means not keeping it separate from your understanding of yourself as a Christian. Many times people want to keep their sexuality separate from their spiritual life. Their sexual desires are so strong that they feel that they must allow them to be satisfied. The Bible has it otherwise. "Shun fornication! Every sin that a person commits is outside the body; but the fornicator sins against the body itself. Or do you not know that your body is a temple of the Holy Spirit within you, which you have from God, and that you are not your own? For you were bought with a price; therefore glorify God in your body" (1 Corinthians 6:18–20).

2. *Refrain from sexual relations that hurt others.* This means maintaining a monogamous relationship that, again, keeps sexuality in its proper place. Sex is a powerful drive that arouses strong emotions. This is one reason, I believe, that reasonable sexual restraints are found within the Bible. Refraining from adultery is not just an idea put into place to frustrate us. It also keeps us from going at one another's throats. I know

people whose lives have been literally destroyed because their spouse committed adultery. This is not to say that a relationship or a marriage cannot recover from infidelity, but the amount of pain and hardship hardly seems worth it.

3. *Always enter into discussions about the sexuality of others not with a sense of judgment, but with compassion.* Another aspect of sexuality is that it incites strong feelings of condemnation. Good people can be quick to condemn others for sexual indiscretions. Even though sexual immorality is a sin, it is equally a sin to spend your time hating others for their practices. Our Savior and model, Jesus Christ, was not one to criticize others for immorality. "Let anyone among you who is without sin be the first to throw a stone at her," Jesus said when he encountered an angry group about to stone a woman accused of adultery (John 8:7). When the group dispersed as a result of this challenge, Jesus said, "Woman, where are they? Has no one condemned you?" She said, "No one, sir." And Jesus said, "Neither do I condemn you. Go your way, and from now on do not sin again" (John 8:10–11).

The model here is not to condemn, but to uplift. Compassion and encouragement are the answers.

4. *Where you have been wronged by someone else, find a way to respond not with anger or jealousy, but with forgiveness.* This is perhaps the most difficult of the practices to follow here. If we have been wronged by someone due to sexual immorality, it is easy for us to

be consumed with "righteous" indignation. The problem is that it may become our life's cause. While it is certainly necessary to go through a process of pain and grief as a result, it is not helpful for the entirety of life to be consumed by it. There comes a point when it is necessary to move on. We can't do this by carrying around the baggage of jealousy and hatred.

Hatred and Anger

Hatred and anger can certainly come from sexual immorality and jealousy, but they can arise from other sources as well. An acquaintance of mine I'll call Andrew is consumed by anger. After fifteen years with an organization, Andrew was told that his management position was being eliminated. First he was given ninety days to find another job. Within a week, however, he was told that a lower-level position had opened up and that he had the choice of either taking this job or leaving the company.

Even though the pay reduction is fairly small, Andrew feels the sting of having lost the prestige of his management position. He is angry all the time: angry with his employer, angry with the manager who "did this" to him, and angry with company executives whom he sees as ultimately responsible. Consumed with what he feels is justifiable anger, he will tell practically anyone he meets about how he has been wronged.

The truth is that Andrew has always been given to anger. It was responsible for the breakup of his first marriage. His children have a hard time with him because he is harsh and overly critical.

Such an angry temperament as Andrew's not only makes a person hard to live with but leads to health problems as well. Recent studies suggest that a tendency toward anger and hostility has grave physical consequences. As Daniel Goleman writes concerning these studies in his recent book on emotional intelligence, "Being prone to anger was a stronger predictor of dying young than were other risk factors such as smoking, high blood pressure, and high cholesterol."[1] Similarly, cardiologist Bruno Cortis, in his book on the psychological aspects of heart disease, cites studies showing that the higher the hostility in a person's psychological makeup, "the higher the incidence of heart attacks and mortality."[2]

The difficulty with anger is that the world is going to give each one of us reasons to be angry. There are always going to be people who put us down and circumstances that don't go our way. You can't really say, though, that a person who has a constant sense of anger about them is a very graceful or God-filled individual. Hence Saint Paul's listing of hatred and anger as among those things indicating a sinful nature.

It is worthwhile to look at yourself and see how prone to anger you are. I encourage you to take a look at your "justifiable" anger too. You might be mislabeling what is generally a hateful nature.

Jealousy

Jealousy comes from fear. I know a young woman whose husband lives in fear, and he makes her life difficult. Although both were only eighteen when they married as a result of her pregnancy, their marriage started out well enough. They had the support of both sets of parents and were affectionate toward each other. He had always had a jealous streak, but nothing really out of control. Things got worse, however, when she took a job. He started to worry about all the things she would be doing and the men that she would be seeing. He started calling her as often as he could throughout the day and interrogated her when she arrived home from work in the evening. Unfortunately, he is bringing about exactly the kind of behavior he does not want to see. Thinking that he is already suspicious of her anyway, she is becoming flirtatious and keeps many of her male friends a secret from her husband. She seems destined to have an affair eventually.

So many difficulties come out of a less than "graceful" temperament. Of course, sometimes jealousy is appropriate. It does allow two people to communicate to each other what they feel is acceptable and unacceptable in their relationship. But the best thing is for a couple to arrive at this decision together, without the rising tide of anger getting in the way.

Jealousy is one of the most destructive of emotions, and it should be handled with care. As with anger, it is helpful to remember that jealousy is one of those characteristics that Saint Paul indicates are the mark of a sinful nature. A constantly jealous person is not living within the kingdom of God.

Perhaps you are prone to jealousy. If so, you may have to ask whether the jealousy you experience is something that gets you out of balance not only in your relationships with others but with your own experience. If it keeps you from experiencing the kingdom of God, is it worth it?

Rage

Rage is anger or jealousy gone out of control. A striking example of this occurred close to where I live. A few years ago a man named Jason went to a party given in honor of his daughter's graduation from kindergarten. Jason's daughter lived with his ex-wife and her new husband, David. During the course of the evening, Jason and David got into an altercation involving a minor incident. Still jealous over the recent marriage, Jason flew into a fit of rage and pulled out a gun he'd brought with him. He was able to calm down after a minute, though, and left the house for his car. David stepped out of the house a few seconds later, standing at the doorway to make sure Jason was leaving. Upon seeing David, Jason, who was just about to open his car door, became angry and pointed his gun at David. By now David had armed himself and shot Jason through the chest. From her bedroom window the daughter watched in horror as the force of the bullet slammed her father against the car, dropped him to his knees, and finally to the ground. He died on his way to the hospital.

Daniel Goleman refers to such outbursts as emotional hijackings. They need not end so violently as this one, but they do involve the temporary short-circuiting of reason in the name of a powerful emotion. Goleman points to the power of rage, saying that of all the moods that people want to escape, "rage seems to be the most intransigent." It seems that anger has a seductive quality. It creates a "self-righteous inner monologue" that propels it along and fills the mind with "the most convincing arguments for venting rage." Unlike what happens when a person experiences an emotion such as sadness, Goleman finds, anger turned to rage is "energizing, even exhilarating."[3]

A fit of rage, fueled by self-righteous indignation, is often a powerful negative force, leaving emotional and physical destruction in its wake. It is a torrent that we easily jump into, but one that will take us far from the kingdom of heaven.

Envy

Dissatisfaction, like anger and jealousy, often becomes a way of life. We all want a little more, whether it be more money, a bigger house, or a better physique. Part of this dissatisfaction lies in the unpleasant feeling we have toward those who have something we want.

Our society does not help in this regard. Although we claim to be living in the land of opportunity, we reserve our praise for the especially remarkable. As theologian Diogenes Allen remarks, "Our society reserves high praise for only the exceptional, those who are at the top or near the top of their profession or endeavor. So almost everyone else has to wrestle with the idea that they have not achieved as much as they ought in a society that claims to offer everyone the opportunity to get to the top."[4]

One result of this unfortunate tension is envy. The problem is that it leads to negative feelings toward the objects of our envy. We feel we have to put down the person who has gotten what we would like to have. "They don't deserve what they got," we might say. Or we might try to find some negative justification for why they have what they have: "I'd be well off too if I were willing to do *that*."

Envy is characteristic of a sinful nature because it easily turns to bitterness. We can't be blissful if we have negative emotions toward others, and it is difficult to live harmoniously with others if all we can think about is what they have and we don't. And if we are constantly thinking about how much more someone has, how much better educated they are, or how they have always seemed to get the breaks in life, we are clearly not focusing on Christ.

Destructive Ambition

Last on our list is destructive ambition. Having come of age during the Watergate era, I and my generation don't have to search very far to see the results of this. *Blind Ambition,* written by Watergate co-conspirator John Dean, became one of the more popular accounts of how the quest for power and influence resulted in the downfall of otherwise talented people.

The political realm, however, is not the only place where destructive ambition plays itself out. Eric, for example, was a young up-and-coming junior executive. At just thirty-two, he once boasted that he was the youngest assistant vice president with his company. He has always been a quick study and learned quickly as a new manager, for example, that taking as much credit as possible for the work of his people was one sure way to look good. It didn't really matter that his employees became dissatisfied and often complained. No one really listened to "the little people" anyway. He also found out that, should he encounter any resistance either from inside or outside his staff, he could easily overcome it by smear tactics. He discredited one of his employees who questioned the direction in which he was taking the unit by trumping up a series of performance problems. She eventually quit to avoid termination. He also "picked off" a challenger from outside his staff by questioning the woman's moral character, even though his evidence was sketchy at best.

Unfortunately, things didn't end up too well for Eric. He began to feel that he was so important that he could take company funds for his own personal use. Didn't he have a right to do this, after all, since he gave so much of himself to the company? Didn't they really "owe" a person of his caliber?

The financial discrepancies were soon discovered. This, along with his poor treatment of others, caused him to be terminated, and he had to start his career all over at a significantly reduced salary. He was lucky that the company didn't prosecute him and put him in jail.

Eric's story isn't a happy one. It's not all that uncommon, either. Different versions of the same story happen all the time. We all know people who get so caught up in their own ambition that they end up being uncaring and unethical human beings. The really sad thing, though, is that they fail to understand the important things of life. The rewards of leading a caring life are something that won't be found on the pages of *Forbes* or the *Wall Street Journal*. They are found, however, in your heart.

Self-Control

These six actions are, in general, those of a nature that lacks control. In fact, when Saint Paul lists the fruits of the Holy Spirit in his letter to the Galatians, he includes self-control. Through the Spirit, we are enabled to lead lives that are firmly anchored. Without the Spirit, we are likely to sail perilously on the Sea of the Self.

In the next chapter we will look at some specific ways of dealing with the passions and emotions that keep us from leading a loving existence. These are ways that begin to help us stay afloat during times of trouble.

The Journey: Finding Your Storms

Before embarking on a trip, it would be helpful to know what the weather patterns are. Such information is easy enough to get. You factor in the time of year and look at the weather records for that time in previous years. You also plan for the difficulties you might face, taking along whatever lifesaving gear you may need.

You can do the same with regards to your emotional life. What is likely to cause emotional problems, and how can you prepare for them? Look at your individual nature. What, in particular, disturbs you the most, and how can you prepare for such a disturbance? Below are three sets of questions designed to help you assess your emotional weather patterns and find ways of dealing with them both psychologically and spiritually. Take a few minutes to ponder them.

1. Looking at your past and present experience, what are the emotional issues that cause you the most difficulty (anger, jealousy, etc.)? What do such emotional issues say about you? How can you prayerfully deal with these issues?
2. When have you felt successful in dealing with emotional events (in other words, when you appropriately "kept your cool")? How were you able to do this? How can you continue to do this in the future?
3. What are some upcoming events that are likely to cause you difficulty? How might leading a more Christ-centered life help you navigate such difficulties?

THREE

Calming the Waters

I n the last chapter we explored the actions of a sinful
nature. We looked specifically at sexual immorality, hatred and anger, jealousy, rage, envy, and selfish ambition. These were discussed individually, although
it is clear that many times they work together. People
can even go through times when all six are at issue.

The real problem is that we are all inclined to sin.
Saint Paul explicitly says that these qualities are the
works of the flesh. All of us, as a result of being flesh,
must face these temptations. Every one of us, Christian and non-Christian, must struggle with the desires
of the flesh. Even though we would like to exhibit the
Spirit-filled qualities of love, patience, gentleness, and
self-control, we are not going to be able to all the time.
We have sexual desires that go beyond our marriages,
we exhibit the qualities of envy and jealousy, and we are
even given to tirades and fits of rage.

Diogenes Allen discusses our fallen nature in an interesting and informative way, focusing on our separate-

ness as it adds to the problem. We cannot expect to get past our individual imperfections to the ground of pure love for any great length of time. We all have limitations. As a result, Allen says that we have to be careful about seeking to live in glory before our time. We want to get there, but "we forget the enormous depths of sin, the frightful power of that boundless horizon that is ourselves." We have to "come to terms with the knowledge that we are egocentric persons and that we are going to remain so throughout this life. Even a saint does not remain in a perpetual state of love, but feels the pressure of other people and powers and the bodily and psychic forces over which no one has control, that draw a person back into the position where all is seen from a self-centered perspective."[1]

The constant pull of temptation, compounded by the difficulty of seeing beyond our individual psyches, is the struggle of our lifetimes. It is the wind feeding the storms that blow through everyone's life, even the lives of "good" people.

Sherry, for example, is a dedicated Christian and, vocationally, a project analyst for a financial institution in the Northeast. Approaching forty years of age, she has held a number of midlevel professional jobs but has never really been able to advance. She feels she has a lot of talent, but she doesn't really have the financial background that would help her to move ahead. Her master's degree in education, even though earned at a prestigious institution, hasn't really qualified her for advancement in her field. She could try to pick up the necessary background by going to school at night, but with a young family she just doesn't have the time. As a result, she often finds herself resenting those who were once her peers but have moved up the corporate ladder much more quickly than she.

Her family focus also seems to limit her opportunities. She notices that the company favors those who work late into the evening five days a week and are even willing to come in on Saturday as well. This means that either single people, people without children, or those with a spouse not working outside of the home tend to be selected for higher jobs.

Still, Sherry recently experienced a stroke of good luck. She is bright and good at what she does, and her recent efforts on a project came to the attention of a couple of the vice presidents on the "seventh floor," where the executives reside. One in particular really feels that Sherry has a lot to offer and even recommended her for a management position. Although ordinarily this would be a real boost for Sherry, there are complicating factors.

To begin with, the position reports to someone Sherry isn't really crazy about, and the feeling seems mutual. John, the manager of the available position, is one of those hard-charging people who doesn't have much use for those who are not totally dedicated to their jobs. He has commented that when he comes in at 7:00 A.M. every morning he can't understand why there aren't more cars in the company parking lot. And when he leaves at 7:00 P.M. he is equally baffled by the scarcity of cars.

Sherry suspects that John sees her as another one of

those "less than committed" types. Additionally, Sherry suspects that she is a little too caring and compassionate for John's taste. He seems to like people who make cut-and-dried comments without a lot of equivocation. Because Sherry tends to look at and understand both sides of an issue before making a decision, and even then tries to incorporate all sides as best she can, she fears that she appears to be less than deliberate in her comments. Sherry bets that John can't understand what the vice president sees in her. He seemed reluctant in the phone call inviting her to interview with him and a little cool when she ran into him in the hallway later that day. Sherry fears that John will be forced to take her and that at some point John will exact vengeance upon her as a result. The working conditions might not be that great under John, and she can't expect the vice president to have enough time to intervene.

John's perceived reluctance is only part of Sherry's problem. Sherry is married to a forty-three-year-old newspaper editor named Hal, who has become increasingly dissatisfied with his job and is interested in making a career change. Having grown up watching *Perry Mason* and other legal shows, Hal has always wanted to practice law, and about a hundred miles away is a college with a well-respected law school. Attending the school would require a lot of time and expense, to say nothing of the lost income that the family would incur. Sherry's promotion would be just enough to make up the difference, and she feels obligated to take the position so that Hal can pursue his education.

But there is yet another issue. Prone to jealousy, Sherry worries about her husband's being away from home to attend school. She knows that Hal has a flirtatious nature and that women respond to him. They have had a few confrontations over this during their twelve years of marriage. Though Hal has always managed to soothe Sherry's fears, she still has enough doubt about him to wonder if his spending time at law school would be the right thing for their marriage. She sees him falling for a young, pretty law student and marrying her after his legal training is over. The mere thought of this makes Sherry's blood boil.

All of this is to say nothing of Sherry's concern over supervising people for the first time in her career. She may also need to arrange child care for their two children should Hal decide to attend law school and she have to work late into the evening.

This storm Sherry is facing results in an unpleasant argument with Hal. Coming home just two nights before her scheduled interview with John, Hal expresses his hope that Sherry will do well in the interview and get the job.

"Well, I guess that would give you what *you* want," Sherry says.

"What do you mean by that?" Hal replies.

"You only want me to have this job so that you can go ahead with your interests. You don't care what I want."

"I thought that this *was* what you wanted."

"I don't know what I want. I just know that this will

give you a chance to go out and do what you want to. I'm sure you'll have lots of fun being back in college, like a kid again. I'm sure your libido will finally have its way."

"That's not what this is about at all. I've just always wanted to be a lawyer. You know that."

"Right," Sherry says sarcastically. "And if you meet someone else while you're up there, so much the better."

Sherry storms out of the house and goes for a drive. When she returns, she and Hal hardly speak a word for the rest of the evening. Sherry feels angry but also embarrassed about her fit of rage. Hal hadn't done anything to deserve that. On his part, Hal feels guilty. He worries about whether he has put his own interests above those of Sherry and the children. Going to law school just may not be a good idea, now or ever. And he remembers the times when, earlier in their marriage, he was a little too flirtatious with other women. He wishes Sherry would see that the flirtations came to nothing and that now he has discontinued them completely.

The next day Sherry is emotionally on edge. She didn't get much sleep the night before because of the confrontation. She is filled with doubt about the possibility of the new position. She really doesn't want to let the vice president down, nor does she want to deprive Hal of the possibility of pursuing a career that is of more interest to him. Still, she doesn't relish the idea of working for someone who seems so much opposed to her. She has experienced this in the past and knows that it usually leads to difficulties. Additionally, she knows that she will have to work a lot more hours, and that troubles her. The part of the day that she enjoys most is spending time with her two children during the early part of the evening. She feels that she will have to say good-bye to this. And the jealousy issue will be there with Hal, whether she likes it or not.

What are some remedies for this situation? Two overlapping approaches can help Sherry sort things out and bring her to a happier, more loving existence. The first is a psychological approach, the second a spiritual one. The first allows space, the second grace.

Let's begin with the psychological approach. In his recent book *You Can Be Happy No Matter What*, Dr. Richard Carlson outlines a program for enhancing what he refers to as "healthy psychological functioning." This is the feeling we experience when we are not bothered by events or otherwise in emotional turmoil. It is a "positive feeling state that exists for no apparent reason." Children, Carlson says, are often in this state of mind because they experience life "simply, without putting too much negative thought into it. When they do experience negativity or frustration, they are able to let it go quickly and return to their natural state of happiness."[2]

We adults also experience this state of mind. It might be while sitting outside on our front porch, enjoying the fall colors, or taking a walk along the beach. Healthy psychological functioning is present "whenever you feel wonderful for no particular reason."[3] It is a state of relaxation and joy.

Important in Carlson's work is his separation of

healthy psychological functioning from the particular situations we are facing. It is not the situations we encounter in life that cause problems but our reactions to them. We don't need to be looking at the autumn trees or the ocean to be happy. Such external events may seem to provide us with a minute of relaxation to clear our minds and enjoy life, but we can have joy independently of seeing the trees or hearing the ocean. Emotions are internal events.

Emotions are influenced by thought, or by our reaction to what we see before us, rather than by the objects or events of the world. Carlson puts it this way:

> It's our *thinking,* not our circumstances, that determine how we feel. We forget, moment to moment, that we are in charge of our thinking, that we are the ones doing the thinking, so it often *appears* as though our circumstances are dictating our feelings and experience of life. Consequently, it seems to make sense to blame our unhappiness on our circumstances, which makes us feel powerless over our lives.[4]

We can, according to Carlson, have a great deal of power with respect to our emotional lives. Carlson identifies a particular tendency of people to analyze situations and to worry about them continuously. He reminds us, though, that it is not the situations themselves that make us sad or depressed, but our reaction to them. "Our level of happiness seems to go up and down with circumstances," Carlson writes. "In reality, it isn't the circumstances, but our interpretation of them that determines our level of well-being."[5] If we can take our attention off whatever is bothering us, we can experience a happy and positive feeling. We can return to the healthy psychological functioning felt at other times in our lives.

This powerful insight can be helpful even in especially troubling situations. Carlson recounts his own experience. A close friend was killed in an automobile accident on the way to Carlson's wedding. Most people would feel obliged to be depressed in such a situation. Instead of feeling sorry for himself, however, Carlson was able to experience a sense of "tremendous gratitude for having known such a wonderful friend."[6] This feeling is a direct result of Carlson's decision to deal with a tragic situation in a positive way.

Carlson has much to say about the attainment of healthy psychological functioning. Suffice it to say that he goes much deeper than telling us we can control our reactions to events (which was the overly simplistic approach I mentioned in the introduction). Carlson explores ways we can have greater influence our over reactions to events. Two of Carlson's methods have direct application to situations such as Sherry's.

The first is the recognition of separate realities. Each of us lives, to an extent, within a separate reality.[7] We have wants and needs that are specific to us. Many times we require that everyone else, particularly the significant others in our lives, share these same concerns. When it becomes apparent that they don't, friction and stress occur.

Sherry and John are obviously not on the same page when it comes to work. Sherry believes that working hard for eight hours a day, and still preserving enough time and energy for her family, is the best she can do both for herself and the company. John feels that a person owes much more to an employer. He expects employees, and especially managers, to be totally committed to the company that provides them with so much.

While we will have more recommendations for Sherry later, for now it seems evident that she needs to reach some kind of agreement with John if she is to work for him. She needs to talk openly with him about her concerns and have John give an account of his. Together they may be able to reach some common ground on how they can successfully work together.

Sherry might also follow Carlson's advice to live within the present moment.[8] As Carlson explains, we frequently "over worry" about events, thinking about them even during times when it would be more beneficial simply to relax and take our minds off everything. By focusing on the present moment, we can take advantage of such times. If I awaken in the middle of the night, worrying about something, what good does that do? Most of the time I am not going to resolve the problem but will only lose sleep and feel even worse the next day. It is more effective simply to focus on the present and enjoy the warmth of my bed than to worry about some event at work or home.

It might seem "natural" for Sherry to worry about her momentous decision all day and night, but continuous attention to her dilemma will not help her solve it. If she can allow herself to live in the present moment—to take a mental break from the issues troubling her—she will be able to come back to the issue refreshed later on. It may be difficult to let go of the problem, but all she need do is look around, see that there are no immediate threats, and relax.

Many people, like Sherry, experience depression because of stress and the tendency to "ruminate" on events, to use psychologist Martin E. P. Seligman's term.[9] Carlson's approach is one means of easing this depression. The separation of event and thought is something that most people will have to spend some time perfecting. It takes time to recognize our differences with others and learn to resolve them from our "separate realities." It also takes practice to learn to live within the present moment and not to allow life's difficulties to become bothersome.

As helpful as this approach is, there is a powerful spiritual supplement. It's helpful, as a means of introducing this supplement, to return to the perspective of Diogenes Allen mentioned near the beginning of this chapter. We are, recall, fallen individuals who can never get beyond our separateness. Consequently, it may not be entirely possible for Sherry and John, for example, to work things out to their mutual satisfaction. Each has individual attitudes and views that have taken years to develop, and with which they may have to struggle for the rest of their lives. Carlson's helpful and commonsense approach notwithstanding, no psychological method is going to lead anyone to perfection, or even to experience perfect peace all the time.

Carlson's approach does, however, open the door so that we can experience the loving healing of our Savior. Once she clears her mind of constant worry, Sherry can call on Jesus and feel his calming peace. (Sherry can, of course, do this independently of Carlson's technique. The point here is these techniques are helpful in providing a breather for us so that we can refocus and remember our Savior.)

Calling on Jesus involves no difficult spiritual practice. It is as simple as just calling to him, and prayer is our way of reaching out to Jesus and receiving his peace. Reading the Scriptures, too, provides deep solace. Listen, for example, to these comforting words:

> "Come to me, all you that are weary and are carrying heavy burdens, and I will give you rest" (Matthew 11:28).

> For God so loved the world that he gave his only Son, so that everyone who believes in him may not perish but may have eternal life (John 3:16).

> The saying is sure and worthy of full acceptance, that Christ Jesus came into the world to save sinners (1 Timothy 1:15).

> If anyone does sin, we have an advocate with the Father, Jesus Christ the righteous; and he is the atoning sacrifice for our sins, and not for ours only but also for the sins of the whole world (1 John 2:1–2).

Such quotations remind us that God loves us totally despite our flaws and our circumstances. These words reassure us that we can experience the joy of eternal life now, in the present. With such a blessing, how can the concerns of the world oppress us?

We can experience peace that extends beyond the instances when we put our difficulties aside. We can experience peace even in the midst of conflict. This comes through allowing Christ into our life in a very deep sense. Knowing that God loves her and Hal despite their failures can keep Sherry from experiencing the "emotional hijacking" we spoke of in the previous chapter. She will have a greater chance of speaking calmly and lovingly to Hal about her concerns, and this increases the chance that together they will come to a more amenable solution. The same is true of her working relationship with John, if in fact the job is offered to her and she accepts it. It's possible for them to establish a way to work together, particularly if at least one of them (Sherry) approaches the situation in a loving way.

But what if after coming to an agreement Sherry takes the job and then John begins to belittle her? To begin with, Sherry can, remembering the first of the Scriptures quoted just above, lay her burden upon Christ and be refreshed. Beyond this, she can experience the transforming power of Christ by taking the perspective of eternity and realizing that this situation is not all that there is. As Saint Paul wrote in his letter to the Galatians, "I have been crucified with Christ; and it is no longer I who live, but it is Christ who lives in me" (2:19–20). This is not to say that she cannot stand up for herself or deal directly with John's belittlement. However, Sherry doesn't have to feel inadequate or depressed because of his treatment.

I have gone some way toward identifying ways to relieve the stress Sherry is under. And in times of difficulty, we might all follow this advice, which springs from both secular and spiritual sources:

1. Realize that your emotional reactions don't have to follow from your circumstances.
2. Understand that the way others see things is not necessarily the way you see them.
3. As much as possible, live within the present moment without worry.
4. Experience peace in all moments through the love of the Savior.
5. Open yourself to this love through prayer and reading of the Scriptures.
6. Act in all things with the grace and peace of Christ.

Still, what ought Sherry to do? Should she pursue the job or not? There are pluses and minuses regardless of the way she chooses. There is no perfect solution, as with many choices in life, no clear route for Sherry to take, nothing from a spiritual perspective telling her what decision to make. And no one else can answer the question for her anyway. She might pray for guidance or look for signs of God's will, but this approach, while helpful, misses some of the point of Christianity. The issue here is not making a perfect choice. It is, rather, serving God in whatever choice is made. Do we expect God to "serve us" by placing us in situations that make us the most comfortable, or even in situations that necessarily make the best use of our skills? On the contrary, we are here to serve God and others in the situations in which we find ourselves.

Whatever path we take, we should travel it with a loving heart filled with the joy of Christ. Many times there are no "right" or "wrong" choices as we make our journey through life. What we do have is the obligation, which is our joy, to journey with Christ.

The Journey: Experiencing Calmness

Calmness is a behavioral response that can be learned. Go through a day and write down the moments when you felt the most calm. What were your thoughts at the time? Once you have examined these times, try to expand this calmness by thinking these or similar thoughts at other points during your day. In effect, you are teaching yourself to be calm by applying thoughts that work for you. Finally, spend a day making this calmness even more profound by experiencing the grace and love of Christ within your already peaceful thoughts.

FOUR

Applications: Messages to the Heart

B efore taking a deeper journey into centering the heart, let's take a look at how a heart-changing experience might take place. The following may be a somewhat fanciful tale, but please read it with the understanding that our experience of life is intimately involved with our attitudes and emotions—that is, with our hearts. Acknowledging Christ changes the heart and influences our experience in ways both small and profound.

Imagine that you are just starting your day. You get up early in the morning, as you always do, and start the rush to get the kids ready for school and yourself ready for work. Throughout this bustle, your attention keeps returning to a tree in your front lawn. You can see the tree come into shape as the sun slowly rises, but there is something unusual about it this morning. There is an object hanging in it, some unusual shape. You want to ignore it because there is so much that needs to be done. The children have to be herded along as they are still drowsy from sleep. The cereal has to be poured and the juice glasses filled. Still, the object in the tree is compelling.

Finally, you can resist the urge no longer. You open the door and step out into the brisk autumn air. You walk toward the tree and see that the shape is a piece of paper. You carefully remove it and try to read the writing scrawled across it, but there still isn't enough light. You walk inside and, as the children are arguing over something at the table, read the writing. It says:

> This is the first of three messages. Today's message is this:
> *Love God in spite of yourself.*

You find this message extremely puzzling. You wonder how it got into the tree. You guess it must have been left for someone else at a neighboring house and simply blew in from somewhere. You absentmindedly fold the paper and push it into your front pocket as you continue to help the kids.

The kids irritate you as you are driving them to school. They get into minor disputes. At the end of your rope, you shout at them to be quiet. You're a little too harsh, you think. Their feelings are hurt. You apologize, feeling the piece of paper in your pocket.

After you drop the kids off you get caught up in traffic. You are trying to cross a particularly difficult intersection and the driver of another car is "foolishly" blocking your ability to get across when the light changes.

"Jerk!" you say as you finally manage to maneuver around him.

The paper in your pocket scratches against you.

You take note of several other incidents throughout the day, situations in which you either react from your own limited understanding or blatantly ignore what you know would be a better way to act. You say a few unkind words about an absent coworker and get angry with an employee who didn't understand your directions and failed to give you exactly what you asked for. You worry, too, when you hear that someone higher up in the organization is unsure of you, thinking that this is the most unfortunate thing that could happen. Your thinking changes, however, as you remember the message in your pocket. Perhaps it *was* meant for you.

As we begin to reflect upon ourselves with the hope of experiencing a changed heart, one thing we will encounter again and again is ourselves. No matter how hard we try, our failures will always be tugging at us. The message found in the tree encapsulates this idea, expanding on the previous chapter's spiritual advice in that it allows us to recognize this "fact" and opens the way for us to put it into perspective.

If you can see yourself at all in the above situation, you know that your imperfections will crop up throughout the day. They will come up at home just when you think you have everything, yourself included, under control. And they will arise at work too, reminding you that no matter how professional you might be, you are still human.

Our imperfections can easily cause us to take some wrong turns. On the one hand, we might become so despondent about them that we give up all hope of leading a spiritual life. We may become depressed or angry. How can we feel good about ourselves spiritually when we hurt others or make such blatant mistakes? We echo the frustration of Saint Paul's cry: "For we know that the law is spiritual; but I am of the flesh, sold into slavery under sin. I do not understand my own actions. For I do not do what I want, but I do the very thing I hate" (Romans 7:14–15).

On the other hand, we may take our imperfections too lightly. We may get into the habit of saying, "Well, I'm not going to be able to come close to my ideal of a spiritually developed person, so I'll just give up." Such a sentiment can quickly result in a lackadaisical attitude toward our spiritual life and can prevent any spiritual development from taking place. It also opens the way up for us to accept our own sins as inevitable.

The remedy for both of these attitudes is to love God in spite of our imperfections. Doing so allows us to understand that while we may be prone to snap at our children when stressed, for example, we need not become overly despondent about it. Neither should we give up trying to be better parents, either. We simply recognize instances when we are making mistakes, continue to pray and seek to experience God's love, and improve with the grace of God living within our hearts.

In fact, we can use the idea behind this message as a spiritual exercise. As you go through your day today (or tomorrow, if you happen to be reading this at night), look at the times when you feel you are being less than perfect. When you start to feel that way, remember to love God and carry God's grace within you. This will enable you to apologize when you need to without becoming despondent about having failed.

The day after the message arrived is one of those rare day's that you've decided to take off from work. You sleep a little later than usual, as is your practice on such days. When you get up you go into the kitchen to make some coffee. You enjoy these times when you are alone and can reflect upon your busy life. Even though you have placed the message carefully in the top drawer of your desk at home, you feel that it was a fluke, caught in the tree by chance.

The sun has been up for a half-hour or so, and soon you must wake the children up for school. Since they don't have to go to child care this morning, they, too, enjoy a little extra sleep. Before you awaken them you walk outside to enjoy the weather.

As you sit in the chair on your front porch, you casually glance over at the tree. You notice that there, once again, is a piece of paper swinging from one of the branches. You walk over to the tree and carefully remove the paper. You unfold it and read the following:

Love God in the tensions and contradictions.

Now you are really perplexed. It seems obvious that these messages are meant for you. Twice is simply too much of a coincidence. But what does this mean? "Love God in the tensions and contradictions." You shake your head and put the note in the pocket of your jeans. You're going to have to think about this one.

Soon the children are up, and you drive them to school. On the way you pass several well-known landmarks. There on the left is the house of a friend who is struggling with a drug addiction. He has always been someone you respected and loved. He is smart and extremely loving toward his wife and children, but his addiction to alcohol and drugs is ruining his life. You don't really know how to help him, other than to suggest he get counseling and go to Narcotics Anonymous.

You think about how some of his issues are similar to yours. He set out on one course in life, but for one reason or another things didn't work out exactly as he planned. He got sidetracked, then had a family and other responsibilities that came along. He couldn't deal with the fact that life just doesn't seem to work out exactly the way it should. And he has an addiction over which he seems to have no control. So much promise, yet so many things getting in the way of where he wants to go. Talent and promise should lead to success, but it doesn't always. Life just doesn't run that smoothly.

Next you pass a church that some of your family members attend. It's unfortunate that religion doesn't seem to make them very loving people. They openly condemn others who believe differently from them. Worse, they feel that believing in God will make things always work out right. Those who are a bit down on their luck, they say, have somehow gotten outside of God's favor. You think religion should always bring about more compassion and understanding, but things don't seem to work that way. Another contradiction.

Finally, you pass the house of some former friends. They are people you used to be close to. Just when things were going well for you spiritually, you got into a bad argument with them. They ended up hurting both you and your spouse deeply. There are such hard feelings now that you are sure you'll never be close again. There's just no trust there. Spiritual progress ought to lead to more harmonious relations with people, but this isn't always the case. Another contradiction.

By the time you drop the children off and return home you are amazed at the relevance of the message you received this morning. You reach down and feel it in your pocket. "Love God in the tensions and contradictions." It might as well have read, "Love God in all things," for, indeed, there are so many tensions and contradictions in life. Loving God seems to be the only way of dealing with them.

Perhaps it is because I was trained as a social scientist that I am so fascinated by the contradictions of life and society. Politics, to take my particular branch of social science, certainly has enough of them. We send politicians off to Washington to act in the public interest for our common good and watch as they become so concerned with getting reelected that their finer concerns drop by the wayside.

Deeper still are the contradictions of society. Fairness, virtue, and kindness are often at odds with material and professional success. How do we begin to live peacefully in such a society and such a world? On the one hand, we feel the urge to be virtuous and kind, while on the other, we may feel judged by the "real" world for not making enough money or having enough power. We often feel the stress that the push and pull of this dichotomy creates.

It's easy enough to acknowledge and talk about such issues. In fact, we might spend much of each day lamenting such "facts" as they are seen in the popular realm. The real rub occurs, however, when tensions and contradictions invade our lives. The expectation that our virtuous action will net us rewards in this world causes us no end of frustration. Additionally, even such expectations that religion will always create better, more loving people, and that spirituality will allow us to have more harmonious relations with all people, can lead to difficulties.

Realistically, life will always have tensions and contradictions. That's just the way the world works. Loving God within these is one way—I think the only way—to deal with such issues gracefully. It is a way of continuing to love within the stresses and disappointments of life.

The third day arrives, and you can hardly wait to see what today's message is. You sit outside with a light jacket on, sipping a cup of coffee. You watch as the sun begins to color the sky. You see there in the tree the third message. You walk over and pluck it from the branch and walk back to the porch. You turn on the porch light and read:

Pray life.

Now this is an interesting message. How on earth can one "pray life"? You reflect on what you have learned so far from the other two messages. The first, "Love God in spite of yourself," made sense enough. Like all humans, you have flaws aplenty, and they can easily throw you off. Loving God makes sense because it prevents you from being overcome by your own frailties and keeps you on the spiritual path. The second, "Love God in spite of the tensions and contradictions," also makes sense. Again, it is easy to get caught up in tensions and contradictions and to become depressed or simply distracted from the spiritual. Loving God within these eases the tensions of life and prevents you from being overcome by such things as lost dreams.

But to "pray life"—what does that mean?

You put the thought away as you go back into another busy day. Toward the middle of the day you find yourself stressed and concerned. You were in a staff meeting earlier and made a comment that your boss didn't seem to like. You thought it was a good idea, but it just didn't seem to go over well. Then you got a phone call from someone else who reminded you of something you were supposed to do that you had totally forgotten. You pile through the items on your desk and find, buried at the bottom, the memo that contained the request. How could you have forgotten it!

After a hurried lunch you come back to your cubicle. Your spouse calls, and you get into a small argument about how to get everything done that you need to that week. You hang up a little angry and feeling that there are still some unresolved issues there.

"Pray life," you think as you recall the message from this morning. After all the concerns you encountered today, is this possible? You are concerned about your job, about how you are perceived, and about your relationship with your spouse. How could you possibly "pray life"? Then again, what have you to lose?

You put the note in your pocket and look at your schedule. You have a meeting to attend and then a project to complete in the afternoon. Rather than get stressed about these, however, you decide to include God in your activities. This isn't something formal, you just decide to include a prayer to experience God's presence in all that you do.

As you go through the rest of the day you feel a sense of peace. You are surprised at this. Even when you are criticized during the meeting, you calmly explain your actions and refrain from getting rattled. Nobody really notices this, but you feel better. By the end of the day you feel a deep sense of calm. When you get home you are able to talk things over with your spouse in a calm manner. For a brief moment you are able to put things in perspective and relax.

Praying life grants immediate access to the mystical. The events of any one day are easily overwhelming. We have things happening to us that are out of our control. Beyond that, we have the *fear* of things happening to us. We never know what any one day will bring. Perhaps it will be the expressed disgruntlement of someone who has power over us or a feud with someone whom we once respected.

Praying life allows for a different perspective of these events. It puts us in a relationship with God such that we accept whatever comes. This makes an enormous difference. It also allows us to view everything from the perspective of the eternal. Many of life's more "minor" events, such as someone's disliking us for some reason or our not saying the exact right thing at the exact right moment, will be things we can deal with and, indeed, laugh about. Praying life allows us to experience life with God. It is a means of remembering that we have an opportunity to go through life with God and experience God in all that we do.

Love God in spite of ourselves. Love God in the tensions and contradictions. Pray life. These principles may begin to make sense to the spiritually turned. What better way to move through life?

Life, however, always has its struggles. As I write this I am dealing with the fact that someone broke into my house and took a few personal possessions and—much more difficult to deal with—a large number of blank checks. I discovered this at the bank when I went to make a withdrawal. The teller told me that I had a zero balance in both my checking and my savings accounts. I asked for a printout and quickly discovered that several checks had been forged under my wife's name.

It has been a couple of days since I discovered this. Even though the bank tells us that it will refund us the money for the bad checks and has stopped payment on future checks, our concerns continue. We must bring a copy of the police report to the bank, then wait for the bank to go through its bureaucracy before we will see our money. This, we are told, will take a couple of weeks. In the meantime, forged checks continue to come in, and we have seen a printout of just one day's efforts totaling around $2,000. As the thief has a number of blank checks, we have no idea how long this will last. The bank tells us that we are not personally liable for these checks, but we wonder if the stores will be as understanding. Soon they will start calling us, wondering why we put a stop payment on the checks, many of which were written for several hundred dollars. How will the collection agencies that they inevitably turn such matters over to deal with us? Will they be understanding? Will they think we are trying to scam them? How much of an effort will we have to go through to prove that we are the victims of forgery?

This is to say nothing of the feelings of violation we are experiencing, first from having our house broken into, and again each time a forged check comes in under our name. There is also the anger toward the thief and the desire for revenge. Finally, there is the fear of a recurrence. Even worse, we could become victims of violence.

These are difficult issues to face, and I am tempted to say that they really aren't spiritual concerns. Isn't spirituality something felt when things are going okay? Isn't it something akin to the psychological notion of self-actualization, something to experience when we are well fed and all our security needs are met?

Nothing could be further from the truth. Now is precisely the time for a spiritual perspective. When situations such as this arise, I tend to feel a little out of control. To maintain a focus on God at these times is important, allowing me to experience a measure of calm and peace and to remain rational and make decisions without too much emotion getting in the way. This is of vital importance now.

This discussion brings to mind a final principle that, in a sense, encompasses the other three. The principle is this:

Do what you can while leaving it to God.

It sounds a little contradictory when you look at it. If you truly love and trust God, won't you just leave all your actions to God? As appealing as this idea may sound, common sense tells us that it doesn't work. I can't rely on God to catch the thief or thieves who broke into my home and are writing checks on my account. I have to go to the police for that. The best course of action is to do the practical things: file the police reports and work with the bank. But I can maintain a sense of peace by recognizing God in all of it.

"God helps those who help themselves" is an oft-quoted proverb that is somewhat consistent with this principle. However, an element is missing from the "help themselves" approach: the possibility of experiencing God in all things, of allowing the peace of the Holy Spirit to do its work. "Do what you can while leaving it to God" expresses how we might experience the bliss that we are, through no effort of our own, entitled to. It opens our hearts so that we can be changed, from the inside out, and improve our ability to love God and our neighbor.

The Journey: Searching for Messages

Synchronicity is a notion that comes up from time to time in modern spiritual thought. Synchronicity is the idea that at least some things in life happen for a reason. For example, we may be in a bookstore looking for a particular book and just happen upon another book on an entirely different subject that helps us with a difficulty we are facing. Or we may get a phone call from a friend we haven't heard from in a long time at just the right moment that we need to hear from that person. Similarly, some word may keep coming up during the course of a day, and reflecting upon it, we discover that the word has some particular meaning to us.

Without getting too far into metaphysics, reflect for a moment on the "chance" occurrences in your life. Were there ever any such occurrences that really helped you to deal with a problem or concern? Is it possible to see these as examples of God's grace?

Finally, reflect upon what happened to the character in this chapter. Go through a day and be open to any "messages" that God may have for you. These may be the chance occurrences of the synchronicity mentioned above or merely some revelation that you have in witnessing how you interact with people. Write down any realizations that you have at the end of the day, and act on them the next. In so doing, you are making you own unique journey toward a changed heart.

FIVE

Inside

I t has been estimated that as much as 90 percent of
what we think on a particular day is a repetition of
what we thought the previous day. The movie
Groundhog Day humorously portrayed such "same-
ness." The film's protagonist (adroitly played by Bill
Murray) is forced to live out the same day in his life
(Groundhog Day) over and over again. In one scene he
describes his predicament to a couple of guys he meets
in a bar. He tells them that he feels trapped, forced to
lead the same boring, repetitious day over and over again.
Without knowing his particular circumstances, the two
men agree that their lives are just like that too.

This situation is not necessarily all bad. Imagine what
it would be like to wake up to different situations every
day. Each morning we would have to figure out how to
deal with new people and surroundings. Although this
might be exciting for a while, it would, no doubt, prove
taxing in the long run.

Still, facing the same circumstances, and dealing with

them in the same way, ought to lead to some reflection on the part of Christians. It is far too easy to fall into sinful traps. Here I am thinking about such things as idle gossip or casual slander. Of course, we can easily fall into more serious offenses, like adultery, blind ambition, and rage. Given the repetitiveness of life, these may become true traps. We get accustomed to dealing with the conditions of our lives in one way, to reacting to the world in a particular manner, and have a hard time pulling ourselves out of these habits.

There are a number of ways of dealing with such circumstances. In the previous chapter I used the story of someone picking simple messages from a tree. Loving God in spite of ourselves and within the tensions and contradictions of life are among the saner ways of dealing with the difficulties that we all face. The same is true of praying life and doing what we can while loving God. It is interesting that while we don't find such messages within the branches of our trees every morning, we can discover the "truth" of the messages as we go through our days. We know, for example, that not everything works out in our favor, because bad things happen to us all the time. The best laid plans often fail, and even the best of lives experiences tragedy. So we need to discover ways of dealing with an imperfect life.

The next three chapters represent a meditation designed to get us out of our usual way of looking at things. The first step is to go inside, to blast out of our way of dealing with the world. The next is to begin to think about how to apply changes within that odd complex that is ourselves in relation to the world. The last is to focus solely on the external, to see how to move about in a world that often just won't support the deeper spiritual life that we strive to attain.

Let's begin with the first step, which will comprise the remainder of this chapter. This involves the internal experience of the changed heart. Since this is, in fact, an experience, let's once again use a fictitious situation. Let's suppose that you have decided to spend some time apart from the world. You are, through some turn of events, given a few weeks to reflect upon and change your outlook on life. As you prepare for your time apart, you see that you are too caught up in life's circumstances. Life just isn't much fun anymore. There are too many bills to pay, too many complex situations with which to deal, and simply too many things to worry about. In all of this, you fear that you are no longer the person that you want to be. Hurried, uncaring, and spiritually empty are words that might be used to describe you. You see this, but you don't really know what to do about it.

Life has gotten so difficult that when this time becomes available for you to separate yourself from your current situation, you jump at it. Like the early Christians who went to the desert—the precursors to the modern monastics—you will live alone. You kiss your spouse and kids good-bye and vow to return a better person. They are sorry to see you go but recognize the need for you to get away for a while. They, too, have grown weary of your attitude.

You have selected a retreat that is in a remote valley

several hours away from where you live. There is a cabin nestled against the edge of a field surrounded by forest. The cabin faces a good-sized ridge about half a mile away. Driving to the valley, you think of all the things you'll miss. Beyond your family, whom you will miss terribly, you think of your friends and coworkers. You also think of the projects that aren't quite finished. You even think of your favorite television programs and the novel that you were in the middle of reading.

Finally arriving at your destination, you park your car and begin the long hike to the cabin. Your provisions, which you arranged ahead of time, consist only of fruits, vegetables, legumes, and water. The change in eating habits was something you'd decided beforehand.

After looking around a bit, and preparing and eating a simple meal, you sit back on the small front porch. You do nothing but sit, which is an unusual activity for you. At home there is always something that needs to be done, some task to be completed, some need to be taken care of. The first thing that you notice as you sit is how quiet it is. No cars rushing by, no children playing in the yard. Everything is still. You begin to feel exhilarated within the stillness but wonder if this feeling will last. Will you become lazy? Will you simply spend your time relaxing and sleeping? As your life has been so hectic of late, the urge to do just that will be compelling.

A great deal has been written about solitude lately. We are beginning to fathom its importance in understanding ourselves and our place in the world. As we take this imaginary solitary journey, it is worthwhile to note the issues that would come up early. For one, we would face the dissolution of the social self. There are people and activities to miss. Even the silence, so refreshing at first, might become an irritant. We would probably also think on those daily concerns that often seem so onerous. We might figure out some new way of doing our finances, for example, and become eager to go back into the world to put it into practice.

Drawing from the monastic experience, we also know we would need to get a grip on our basic appetites. These are the bodily desires of food, sleep, and sex. It is interesting how much these desires shape our personal lives, even when we think of ourselves as superior to them. Our desire for food, for example, is so strong that we pattern our days after it. Sleep, too, is something that shapes our days. And sex, at least in our society, has achieved supreme status in terms of how we interact with one another.

The idea is not to overcome these desires and drive them away, for they are a part of human life. The goal (and a lofty one at that) is to achieve a balance with respect to these appetites. First is the need to understand yourself in relation to food—what you will eat and what you won't. This is necessary if you are to experience any kind of discipline in solitary living. Without social interaction, food easily becomes the high point of one's day. Eating can be put in a proper perspective by consuming sensible meals. Next is sleep. Lethargy may well overcome someone who doesn't have the opportunity to interact with others but can be taken care of by determining a schedule and staying with it. Additionally, a schedule of activity will fill the day with something other than rest. Finally, the desire to fulfill the sexual appetite will be strong. Sexuality for the solitary is, of course, going to be problematic, but the goal is to transcend sexuality for the short term and to put it in proper perspective upon one's return to the world.

After a week in solitude, the issues of your new world begin to come to the fore. You have managed to stay with a schedule, and you are beginning to get used to the simple food (though a steak still sounds appealing to you). You have managed to deal with your time by establishing a set pattern of reading the Scriptures, meditating, hiking in the woods, and doing some woodwork. You have, in all this, felt a growing sense of God's presence. Still, you have times of deep despair. You remember some of the things that people have done to you, some of the things that disturb you deeply. The unkind words that your spouse recently said to you come to mind, and you wonder about your relationship. You think, too, about some of the people at work who really get to you, people with whom you will probably never have a good relationship. Finally, you think about the years ahead. What about this life that you have chosen— or, to put it more accurately, that has chosen you? Are you really on the right path? This all causes moments of anger, moments that break into your peaceful moods and create a great deal of distress.

So although the scenery is often breathtaking and the

air invigorating, you are easily disturbed. You wanted to find peace but often experience the opposite. One day, in anger, you take a piece of woodwork that you were completing—a small, intricately carved bird—and throw it against the side of your cabin. This all seems like such a waste!

The tough work of changing a heart is not completed during a simple, trouble-free retreat. To use the metaphor from chapter 2, it involves staying anchored during the swells that come and go in the sea of our lives. In solitude, as in meditation, the experience of the swells is often intensified. After all, we don't have the typical distractions to occupy us. This intensification is, oddly enough, what a retreat or meditative practice is all about. It's not the quick increase of a peaceful feeling that is the goal, although that may appear to be the initial reason. This is why meditation in particular can be a very difficult practice. It brings up all manner of emotions—some peaceful and some disturbing. The real task is undergoing the hard work of experiencing our frustrations and shortcomings (in short, our humanity) and breaking through, occasionally, to the ground of pure love.

You are surprised after a couple of weeks in your "hermitage" by the approach of an older man who, though slightly disheveled, has the look of one possessing wisdom. His hair is long and gray, as is his beard. You guess that he is in his sixties, though he has a young, spry quality that makes his age hard to determine definitively. A little unaccustomed to companionship, you nevertheless call him over for a chat.

"Are you a hiker?" you ask.

"No. I live a few miles from here, up in the hills to the north. Occasionally I come this way to pick some berries that grow just down the trail. I didn't know this place was occupied."

"I'm staying here for a few weeks, a sort of mini-vacation."

"Getting away from it all?"

"You might say that. Is that what you did?"

"Yes—I just decided not to go back. Why did you want to get away?"

"I just thought things were getting too overwhelming." You wonder why you feel so free to confide in this man.

"What was overwhelming?"

"The commitments I had, the need to be successful while at the same time wondering what success really was, the feeling of being trapped."

"Have you come to terms with that since you've been here?"

"Not really. All I feel is that I'll have to go back soon, and I really haven't resolved anything. If anything, things are worse."

"Why?"

"Because I feel the tensions in my life all the more. I feel the stresses I have with my friends and family, the tensions I have in terms of a career, the weight of commitments upon me. I know I have to go back to these."

"Why do you have to go back?"

"Because that's where my life is. Those are the people I love."

"Then why does everything seem so overwhelming?"

You think about this last question for a minute. You are starting to grow tired of the conversation. You are growing weary of all the questions.

"It just does. I don't feel that I can get and keep a proper perspective."

"Why?"

"Because I get too caught up in things," you finally say, after pausing for a moment.

"Why?"

"Because it's my life."

"Is it?"

At this comment the man smiles and walks away.

The word *why* can be a searing one. I recall sitting in a restaurant a couple of years ago, having lunch with someone I had recently met. We got into a conversation about what we would like to do with our lives. I started talking about things I would like to do, such as write, but would immediately say that it was not possible.

"Why?" he asked.

I thought it was fairly obvious. I had a family that depended on me to provide a steady income and the usual number of financial responsibilities. Still, each time I brought up a possible vocation and said I couldn't possibly pursue it, he would ask the same question—"Why?" Soon I felt awkward. I seemed to have all of these justifications, yet there were important things that I wanted to do.

In the conversation above, the simple questions also have a searing quality. Reading through it again, I am reminded of Jesus and his encounter with Satan in the wilderness.

"Why don't you change the stones into bread?" Satan asked.

"Why don't you jump and let the angels catch you?"

"Why don't you attain power and enjoy all of the pleasures of the world?"

Such questions gave Jesus the opportunity to share with us something of his life and his motivations. We, too, go deeper into ourselves—in essence, defining ourselves—through engaging in a conversation so dominated by "why." Why is life so difficult? Why do we let things bother us? Why do we take ourselves so seriously? Why do we get so caught up in the particulars of our lives?

That last question, which is similar to the last one in our imagined conversation with the hermit/hiker, really gets to the heart of the matter. We take ourselves so seriously because, after all, this is the only life we have. It belongs to us, does it not?

Now we are really at the center of things, the core that some of us would call our hearts. This is our only life, we think. It belongs to us. We are responsible for it.

It is this kind of thinking that leads to a lot of anxiety but can also lead to a lot of change. The simple realization that can bring about this change has to do with placing Christ at the center of our existence—giving ourselves to Christ in a very deep sense. In Saint John's Gospel, Jesus puts this in terms of abiding in him. "Abide in me as I abide in you," he says. "Just as the branch cannot bear fruit by itself unless it abides in the vine, neither can you unless you abide in me. I am the vine, you are the branches. Those who abide in me and I in them bear much fruit, because apart from me you can do nothing" (15:4–5).

Abiding in Christ is the means of long and lasting change. Interestingly, the immediate external aspect—bearing fruit—is somewhat easy to discern and will be explored in subsequent chapters. Bearing fruit indicates, I think, outward and visible signs of Christ's work in you. It is the observable aspect of a Christ-centered life.

The internal aspects of abiding in Christ are somewhat harder to explain. They involve a sense of peace but also a sense of completeness, which we will discuss in the next chapter. It is difficult to describe such things because they are best *experienced*. The trick is to experience them within the joys and difficulties of life.

Now in the fourth week of your stay, you've created a pattern for yourself. As you struggle with the frustrations and enjoy the blessings, however, you gain no deeper insights.

One morning, in the middle of chopping wood, you notice how striking the surroundings are. The sky is just starting to clear from the rainy weather of the previous day. A few clouds still hang about the nearby ridge. The air is fresh but still slightly damp. The sight of the field and the hills and the still young morning sunshine, along with the scent of the air, is especially peaceful.

You lay the ax down and sit on a nearby stump. Although you know you have awakened to the same scenery day in and day out for the last few weeks, you are taken by the spectacular nature of it all. It is the beauty in the ordinariness that is especially transforming. You think about the comments from the traveler of several days ago. Is it your life? Like your surroundings, you, too, are part of the scenery. And like the scenery, you owe your very existence to God.

This simple understanding does something to you that is hard to describe. It is as if something within you dissolves for a moment. You no longer see yourself as having monumental importance to the world. The world is not structured for you, you now realize. Rather than disturbing you, this insight provides a great relief. You feel freer, lighter. More important is your sense of enjoyment. Before, what other people thought about you seemed to be of extreme importance. You used to sit and muse about how you looked in their eyes, and your emotional state often depended upon how well others seemed to think you were doing. Now all of that is much less significant.

You pick up the ax and start back for the cabin. It's time to go.

People have had deep spiritual realizations that are of a similar nature to the one described above. The monk Thomas Merton, for example, wrote about a powerful experience he had upon approaching the reclining Buddha and accompanying figures in Polonaruwa, just a few days before his death. His account was published post-humously in *The Asian Journal of Thomas Merton:* "Looking at these figures, I was suddenly, almost forc-ibly jerked clean out of the habitual, half-tied vision of things, and an inner clearness, clarity, as if exploding from the rocks themselves, became evident and obvious." Merton further wrote that he felt he had seen what he had been "obscurely looking for" and had "pierced through the surface," moving beyond the "shadow and the disguise."[1]

Such experiences, though deeply felt, are hard to un-derstand and describe.[2] What does *an inner clearness* mean, for example, or *piercing through the shadow and the disguise*? Much could be written in an attempt to interpret such an experience.

Our concern here, of course, is with changing the heart. An initial step along the way has to be the realiza-tion of God's presence in ourselves, others, and, indeed, all of creation. This may come about through either a sudden experience or awakening, or through a slow growth. Either way, the result is the same: a growing sense of love and completeness, as well as an ineffable feeling of having experienced God in some way. Life will still have its peaks and valleys, of course, but within these will be the continuing stream of God's love.

The "stages" outlined above are those common to many solitary experiences.[3] These are, in fact, fairly commonsensical. There is the experience of needing to get a grip on one's appetites, as well as a sense of the dissolution of the self. Then reflection on life and its seeming meaninglessness follows, resulting in severe frustration. Amidst all of this comes the experience of letting go of the self into God. This is what is meant by a changed heart. It is the surrendering of the self, with all its needs and wants, to Christ.

It is important that such realizations, whether of the initial or ongoing kind, be available to us not just in solitude but in our ordinary walks through life as well. Personally, I struggled for years because I did not feel that I was in the appropriate setting for any kind of fulfillment. As a spiritual person, I sought fulfillment associated with joy and peace. Although availing myself of solitary experiences when time permitted, it was not in such a setting that I finally experienced a sense of peace. It was, rather, through the growing realization that many daily experiences are opportunities for Christ-centered worship. It was the ability to see God in the people and the situations around me that enabled me, finally, to experience something of a changed heart.

While a heart can change in any number of settings, we chose the solitary road simply for illustrative purposes. In any event, one who is concerned with living a spiritually based life cannot avoid this inner process. And it will not be easy: remember, we're talking about transforming a heart already hardened by life's blows. Think of the man I mentioned in the introduction. Devastated by his wife's infidelity and the subsequent end of his marriage, he is in such bad shape that it might be easy to write him off. But nothing could be further from the truth because the love of God is there for him to experience and to help reshape his life. It will not be an easy road, and there are bound to be times of anger and pain, but even he can come to have a centered heart.

God's love for us is easily accessible and utterly transformative. All we have to do is open the door, and remember to keep opening the door, for the rest of our lives.

The Journey: Opening the Door

Take the entire morning of a day that you have off and plan to spend some time alone. Select a nearby place with a natural setting. This might be a park or perhaps a stream that you can walk beside. Go there, and walk along, emptying yourself of your concerns. Once you let go of your worries, fill yourself with the love of Christ through seeing him in yourself and your surroundings. Pause to reflect upon Christ's love opening the door to your heart. Then write down your heartfelt experiences.

SIX

"　—　"

I once saw a Japanese print that left a deep impression
upon me. Half of the painting depicted a hut at
the foot of a mountain range. Leading up to the hut
was a walkway from a path that came off the range. The
central mountain of the range rose majestically above
the scenery into a grayish sky.

The other half of the print was totally blank.

I suppose reams could be written about the meaning
of such a painting. For me it represents the interaction
of the self with life. The Japanese print presents life as
the hut, the path, and the mountain range; but that is
only the half of it. The other half is our own self, the
void we fill with our own way of "looking" at things.
The hut, path, and mountain do not exist for us independent of our own experience. They are what they are
to us because of how we experience them. It is our interaction with the world that comprises our lives.

What might this mean for the Christian? This is the
territory of the "dash" that serves as the title for this

chapter. In looking at ourselves from the inside out—that is, from the interior to the exterior—we are in many respects exploring a false process. We don't experience something first by checking our inside states and attitudes and then moving beyond these to the thing being experienced. We actually experience things all at once. In other words, the interaction of ourselves with the world is very intimate and immediate.

The "false" process of moving from inside out does, however, provide us with an interesting perspective. It allows us to think "as if" we could unbundle this process. It provides us some space to move around within our relationship to the world and determine where some new attitudes might be necessary. Then, applying our discovery to our actual lives, we can alter this immediate experience with a changed spiritual attitude.

Let's begin by returning once more to the internal space of our hearts. In the last chapter we discussed the transformative power that the Spirit provides when we allow God a central place in our lives. There is one aspect of this that is particularly powerful, though only alluded to in the New Testament a couple of times. This is the aspect of completeness. James writes to his brothers and sisters to consider it a joy "whenever you face trials of any kind, because you know that the testing of your faith produces endurance; and let endurance have its full effect, so that you may be mature and *complete*, lacking in nothing" (1:2–4, italics added). Here the notion of completeness is tied to maturity as well as to the feeling of having all that is needed.

A similar use of complete is found in John's first epistle. John says that he is writing the letter to talk about Christ "so that our joy may be *complete*" (1:4, italics added). Here we see that God renders our joy, our happiness, whole.

What does this mean, this sense of wholeness in our lives in general and our joy in particular? Again, this is better experienced than described, but essentially it is the sense that without God our lives are somehow lacking. We feel fragmented, empty. With God we experience a sense of completion and total joy. We know this quite clearly when we notice where our focus is at any given time. If our focus is upon something we want, or on some perceived need, then we will obviously feel a lack of completion. The problem is that there is always a lack of completion. No matter what we have, someone always has a little more. Someone always has a better car or a faster modem, is better looking or in better shape, and so on. The list is endless.

Focusing on Christ, however, is different. When we focus on Jesus, we have a sense of completeness, regardless of what we may want or need. Completeness does not depend on the circumstances we may be in or the situations we may be facing. It is, rather, an aspect of grace, something that we can experience regardless of our "shortcomings."

This sense of completeness is something that we can carry about with us. Here is one area where we can begin to explore the transaction between the changed heart and the world. If I say, for example, that I have a sense of completeness as the result of a heart that is centered on Christ, you would expect certain things from me. Would you not expect to see this manifested in the manner with which I deal with others? You would not expect to find me always wanting, always looking for something else. This would hardly be consistent with the notion of "completeness."

This same perspective may be applied to other marks of the Christian character. Wouldn't it be absurd for someone to say that they experience a sense of love and joy without exhibiting these in their relations with others? Could I say, for example, that I had experienced a sense of God's love, and that this caused me to feel a sense of peace with God and all of creation, and not manifest this as I move about within this creation?

Permit me, as we think through this odd terrain that is no terrain between the internal and external self, to draw upon three related lines of argument. I take these lines from my formal training in the social sciences. The first approach is one I'll simply refer to as the social aspect of spirituality. Although the spiritual experience is often thought of as being a solitary one, there is a public aspect to it as well. Having a religious or spiritual experience will cause us to want to talk about it with other people. This is not only for our own benefit but also to explain to others what has happened. Once we begin to *talk* about a greater or more complete sense of joy, our experience is no longer solitary—it becomes a shared experience.

The second approach to a spiritual experience may be called the linguistic aspect, and it obviously builds upon the social nature just mentioned. The terms used to describe a spiritual experience within the Christian tradition are typically those such as *love, joy, peace,* and so on—what I will call "pointer" terms. Although they may be describing internal states, they immediately bring to mind or point to certain behaviors as well. If I say that I am now filled with a sense of love, you would expect to see in my actions toward others a number of behaviors. You would expect to see me being kinder, more understanding, and more supportive of others. You would not expect to see me harsher, more critical, or angrier toward others. The same is true of joy. If I say that I now have a complete sense of joy, you would expect to see me, quite simply, happier. You would not expect to see me depressed. If I said to you that I had experienced complete joy, yet I was unhappy all of the time, you would wonder about my use of the term. You would wonder if I were using it in some unusual way, or if I really knew what the term means at all.

This brings us to the final relational approach to spiritual experience: the ethical or moral. If I say that I now have a sense of peace and love with the world, yet I engage in what are widely held to be reprehensible behaviors (spousal abuse, acts of violence, theft, and so forth), then those around me are going to wonder about the inconsistency of my acts and my words. Most attempts to reconcile the two are going to involve an explanation of my failure adequately to match my description of my internal state with the way I am acting. I might be called mentally imbalanced or, more simply, a hypocrite. I might be accused of misrepresenting my internal state so that I can gain an advantage over others. In such an instance, I might be trying to win someone's confidence by lying about a religious experience so that I can gain their confidence and then abuse them.

What does this say about a Hitler-type, however, who might claim a vision of love for the human race and a desire to "purify" the race through genocide? Most of us will rightly see such a view as wrong and inconsistent with the very notion of love. Again, we will begin to look for some kind of mental imbalance, some kind of pathology, to understand why someone could be holding such a wildly inconsistent view.

The three related aspects of spiritual experience that have to do with our internal and external actions are, then, the social, linguistic, and moral. They might be depicted somewhat graphically in the movement from inside to out as follows:

$$Social$$

$$Inside \longrightarrow Linguistic \longrightarrow Out$$

$$Ethical$$

The social, linguistic, and ethical relate to how we describe our internal states—how we help others understand the validity of what we are saying. That is, whether what we are saying about ourselves makes sense.

The Bible, interestingly, uses the notion of bearing

fruit to describe what we're talking about here. The idea is that the deep internal change brought about by living within the Holy Spirit will naturally manifest itself both internally and externally. Thus the famous passage from Galatians says that "the *fruit* of the Spirit is love, joy, peace, patience, kindness, generosity, faithfulness, gentleness and self-control" (5:22–33, italics added). Some of these notions have a more internal quality (peace and joy), while others deal directly with one's treatment of others (gentleness and self-control). Again, even with the internal qualities, there is an external element, as was discussed previously under the idea of pointer terms. We would expect to see, then, that a person who has the Holy Spirit living within him or her will exhibit the above characteristics to one degree or another in their actions.

The Letter to the Colossians echoes this sentiment: Saint Paul writes that he has not ceased praying that his readers "may lead lives worthy of the Lord, fully pleasing to him, as you bear fruit in every good work and as you grow in the knowledge of God" (1:10). Here, again, is the idea that leading a life with God as the focus results in the manifestation of good works, which will occur just as plants or trees bear fruit.

As we look inside and out, we expect something new to happen as a result of someone's living within the Holy Spirit. There is going to be a change reaching to the core of that person's being, and this change will show up in her or his relations with others. This can be spoken of metaphorically as "bearing fruit."

A few caveats: For one, this is not a smooth "process." The path of spiritual development is mysterious, difficult, and above all unpredictable. While we can talk about the fruits of the Spirit in a general sense, it is simply true that each person is unique. People have differing gifts, so they will exhibit one or the other of the fruits of the Spirit in differing degrees. Similarly, people have different weaknesses and challenges. One person may have the challenge of a strong-willed and tempestuous nature that will have to be brought under control. Others may have to learn to be more assertive.

Furthermore, grace has its own way of working. Consider such examples as the person who decides, after a long struggle, to become a minister, only to find out the next week that he has terminal cancer. Or the "spiritually advanced" person who is shaken by some event that seems almost designed to bring this supremely good woman to her knees. Such a process as sanctification (that is, becoming a better person in God's eyes) may well necessitate a good deal of suffering. As David Nicholl says in his book on holiness, "It appears that the capacity for self-sacrifice which the saints display only develops in those who have become spontaneous, pure and innocent through joyfully embracing suffering. Most of us, on the other hand, are still very much beginners; we find ourselves neither spontaneous nor pure nor innocent and we shrink from suffering."[1]

The fact is, receiving the Word of God as a seed and having this Word grow within us is an internal process. In anyone's life there are going to be moments of sheer terror when the world seems turned upside down and beliefs and attitudes are shaken to their foundations. Getting through these moments will be difficult and will tend to push a person far below where they want to be spiritually. You often can't use a person's material circumstances, or even the lack of suffering in her or his life, as a measure of spirituality. In the mystery of grace, many times spiritually centered people will emerge from a struggle even further along than they were before, provided they find a way to offer their circumstances to God. In other words, within the moments of terror are the seeds of a deeper experience with God. Being moments of terror, however, they can temporarily prevent us from being open to God.

It is impossible to draw hard, fast, and rigid criteria for the path of spiritual development. We must also remember that we will be unable to be perfect representations of God's love to others. It is helpful to recall Diogenes Allen's thoughts on human nature. We are all, remember, subject to our individual perspectives. This "individuality" is something that we will never be able to get beyond. As Allen writes, "A great deal of our life is spent this way: seeing things from our own point of view, and thereby being out of contact, out of touch, with great and radiant realities all around us."[2]

Though seeing our isolation as problematic and undeniable, Allen, too, argues for a growing sense of the kingdom of heaven through a focus on God. Allen encourages us to practice "attentiveness" to God to experience this kingdom. "It is here," he writes, "in an attentiveness that breaks the illusion of our self-centered fantasy world made up of our false self-importance, that the kingdom of God begins to dawn. The reality of the world begins to emerge as we ourselves begin to experience ourselves as but one reality among many. Then the world's goodness, its fascinating splendor, begins to reveal itself. It is seen as the object of a perfect love—God's."[3]

To bring these thoughts into sharper focus, let's return to the dash at the beginning of this chapter. We have so far been taking the cautious step from an internal change of the heart to the external world of action. We've seen that it is hard to think of an internal change of heart without expecting an external change of action. We tend to think of such change as being a part of a process whereby a person grows spiritually through the acceptance of Christ into their lives and the placement of him at the center. Although this may appear to be a process, it is often not a smooth one, for there will be trials and tribulations along the way, as there tend to be with following any path. So it might be better not to think of a dash here but, rather, of a Spanish tilde which looks like this: ~ .

Rather than having our depiction of the movement from internal change to external actions look like this:

Inside — Out

it is actually a little more accurate to have it look like this:

Inside ~ Out

This helps us to see that the process is not quite linear. This also means that it is difficult for us, from our extremely limited perspective, to draw conclusions about the spiritual development of others. That, I think, is one reason why Jesus was so careful to warn us against judging other people. The process is difficult, and we, ourselves, are undergoing it. We don't have the authority to say definitively whether someone is totally missing the boat spiritually, although we do need to attend to one another and offer loving help where we can.

Let's conclude this chapter by returning to the Japanese print mentioned at the beginning. We are now getting ready, in the next chapter, to step a wary foot into the reality of life. It's as if we are emerging from the nothingness of the print and stepping out into the world. We realize, however, that the metaphor of the Japanese print can take us only so far. It is not that there is a complete separation of us from what we see. There is an intimate relation that we have to attend to. Our views and attitudes from our "insides" will closely relate to what happens in the world. Additionally, we are not stepping into a static, motionless picture. We are actually stepping into a moving reality. Within this reality, we can easily get sidetracked and lost by the constant change around us. It is even easy to lose sight of God.

What to do? The best we can do is keep the faith and realize that this makes all the difference in the world. Donald Nicholl summarizes this attitude well in *Holiness*:

At the very centre of the universe is a loving Heart whose longings are the source of our own hearts' longings. Hence our own longings can never be in vain, because they correspond with reality, with that Heart upon which our universe is centered.

As has already been said, we can never be discouraged so long as we realize this truth; because it means quite literally that not even the slightest honest effort upon our part is ever wasted, but eventually bears fruit. How vital this realization is becomes clear when we reflect upon how many frustrations we experience every day of our lives, as a result of which it can sometimes seem as though our lives are nothing but an endless series of frustrations.[4]

Nicholl goes on to say that it is only by faith that we realize that our frustrations are not in vain. Occasionally a veil is lifted, and we are "granted a glimpse" of how our frustrations do in fact "bear fruit."[5] This gets at what I have been saying from a slightly different angle. It fills out what is meant by faith, and how faith works. To match it with my perspective, if we put God at the center of our beings, just as God is at the center of the universe, then we will begin to experience moments of love and completeness. Once this experience seasons our actions, then we will truly see the miracles that God creates, even within the frustrations and difficulties of life. This is a joyous process.

We stand, then, before reality with our attitudes and perspectives rising within us. As you stand before this reality with the love of God, experience the transcendence of this Presence and act accordingly.

The Journey: Reaction Time

We all have habitual reactions to life's events. These are based upon our values and beliefs. Many of these are often part of an unconscious process. We condemn others, bemoan our circumstances, and quickly form opinions without even thinking about it.

Spend a day short-circuiting this process. Expand your time to react, withholding your reactions to events pending further reflection. Write down the events and then take a look at them that evening. Prayerfully examine how you might react to them from a more Christ-centered perspective. Write your thoughts down, and spend tomorrow acting from your new perspective.

SEVEN

Out

One warm night, sitting on your front porch, thinking about nothing in particular, you notice a man walking down your street. It is a little unusual for someone to be walking around this late at night, so your interest is immediately aroused. There is something peculiar about this stranger, something that you can't quite explain. He seems to engender a sense of peace even from the distance from which you are watching.

You are, nonetheless, surprised at your reaction when he leaves the road and steps onto your lawn. Ordinarily, you would instantly feel apprehensive concerning such an intrusion. You might wonder if the person is dangerous and out to harm you or your family. Such are the times in which we live. Instead, you feel the opposite of apprehension. You experience a calmness, as if his approach were the most natural thing in the world.

The stranger sits down beside you and remains silent for a few minutes. This doesn't bother you at all because you have never experienced such a sense of calm. After a few minutes he finally speaks.

"You will be given a gift. For one day you will have the ability to bring a measure of peace to those around you."

After saying this, the stranger rises and walks away. You go inside, curl up, and fall asleep. You haven't slept this well in years.

You rise early, before the rest of your family, and drive to work. As you drive you think about the stranger's words last night. Could it really have happened, or did you just fall asleep and dream about it?

When you get to work you stop at the desk of the person who is closest to your office, as you usually do, and say a few words of greeting. You notice, however, that you are not quite feeling the same today. As you speak to her, you are not thinking about what you have to do next or when your next meeting is. You are genuinely interested in this person.

She tells you that she is frustrated because she had some car trouble over the weekend and had to take her car to the shop. She is concerned because she doesn't know how much it will cost. You listen for a while and then pass along the name of a good mechanic that you know in case she continues to have problems. She seems a little more relaxed just because someone stopped by and really listened to her.

"Oh, I'm sure that it will be okay," she says. "Just a little inconvenience."

Throughout the day you run into and talk to the usual people. Each time, you notice that you are less concerned

with your own "agenda" and more interested in whom-
ever you are talking to. As you talk to them, you wish
them a sense of peace, and they seem to respond. Even
when you talk to a coworker whom you have known for
a few years and who has disliked you for every one of
those years, you feel none of your usual apprehension.
She may be against you, but that really doesn't matter.
You wish her a sense of peace, and she responds, if only
for a moment. You think about the stranger's statement
that you will be able to grant a "measure" of peace. You
suspect that your coworker, like you on so many occa-
sions, may be too caught up in her own agenda to experience peace for very long.

At the end of the day you feel relaxed and invigo-
rated instead of drained and tired. You think not only
about how you've conducted yourself this day, but how
you've acted on previous days. It seems as if the "power"
you were granted was really no power at all. It was simply a suspension of yourself, or your ego, in the name of
paying attention to others and wishing them peace.

As you go through the next day you notice that as
long as you practice what you've learned, you get the
same result. The person you talk to seems to be a little
more peaceful. There are also times when you are able
to be really helpful and to offer good advice to people.
This gives you a sense of completeness that you haven't
experienced for a long time.

Perhaps someday you, too, will walk down someone's
street, sit next to them, and give them the same "gift."

Jesus, as we know, was asked once about how to obtain eternal life. His response was very simple. Love God and love your neighbor. It is interesting that he did not go into some long theological discourse designed to impress his listeners. Think of what some of today's spiritual leaders might answer to this question. They might say that the key to eternal life is contained in the particulars of one's worship service or in what one does in response to a pressing social issue. Perhaps it might be whether a person has had a particular kind of experience or depend upon the party for which one votes.

Jesus doesn't go that route. The path to eternity is simple. It is traversed by loving God and loving your neighbor.

This gets us directly to the outward experience of being a Christian. It might seem that loving your neighbor is the sole phrase that is relevant to our outward behavior. Actually, the entire phrase is important. Loving God is equally important to leading the outward life of a Christian.

Let's look at this for a minute. It has been said many times that to love someone else it is necessary to love yourself first. A person who hates himself or herself or who fails to see the good within will probably have a hard time seeing the good in others. There is a deeper sense, however, in which loving God helps in loving ourselves and in loving others. This is true for many reasons.

For one, we know that in God, through Christ, we are forgiven for our sins. In accepting this forgiveness we begin to understand that God loves us no matter what. God loves us in spite of the short temper we've exhibited, the lack of concern we've shown, or the "little" lies we tell to get out of jams. Experiencing this love is a powerful means of accepting our own shortcomings and thereby loving ourselves as God loves us.

This leads directly to loving others. Just as we recognize and are wounded by our own sins and shortcomings, we also recognize and are wounded by the shortcomings of others. But we need to remember that God also loves those others with whom we are dealing. They, too, can ask for and receive forgiveness. A changed heart, a nature focused on God, allows us to empathize with them and to do what we can to forgive them and assist them to a greater understanding of God's love. It enables us to love them too.

So while it may be true that you must love yourself before you can love others, there is a more powerful statement to make from a spiritual perspective. Recognizing our own sinful nature helps us to understand the sinful nature of the world around us. Seeing God's love and forgiveness of us also allows us to see God's love and forgiveness of others. This even provides us with a model for interacting with the world. If God loves and forgives others, should we not do the same?

This model is clearly behind the parable of the Unmerciful Servant (see Matthew 18:23–35). Here Jesus tells of a servant who owes his king a lot of money. When the servant begs for mercy, the king graciously cancels the debt. The servant then encounters a fellow servant who owes him money. The servant, however, refuses to cancel this debt and has the other servant thrown into prison. When the king hears of this, he is angry.

"Should you not have had mercy on your fellow slave, as I had mercy on you?" the kings asks as he puts the servant in prison and has him tortured.

"So my heavenly Father will also do to you," Jesus says, "if you do not forgive your brother or sister from your heart" (Matthew 18:35).

Here we see the deep unity in the command to love God and love our neighbor. Jesus could have said, "In loving God, you love your neighbor." It is in loving God that we experience God's love and forgiveness of us, which in turn should lead to our love and forgiveness of others.

There is another sense in which loving God lends itself to loving our neighbor. God ignites within us a sense of compassion. Jesus exhibits compassion time and again. Think of his telling the disciples to allow the children to come to him. Think of his compassion for the family of Lazarus, which led him to raise Lazarus from the dead. Think of his love even for the sinners of the world, whom he cherished so much that he was criticized for associating with the drunk and disreputable. Finally, think of his compassion for the woman caught in adultery, whom others would have stoned to death. He gave her love and forgiveness instead of condemnation and anger.

How might we manifest this divine attribute—this compassion and forgiveness for others—in real life?

The story that began this chapter provides some illumination. We see the main character letting go of his or her agenda and focusing upon the other person. This, in fact, is really letting go of the self, with all of its commitments and concerns. This release of the self sets the stage for a true concern for others, which is a necessary condition for loving one's neighbors.

There is no better statement of this type of selfless love than the Peace Prayer attributed to Saint Francis of Assisi. The prayer, as most of us know, goes like this:

> Lord, make me an instrument of your peace.
> Where there is hatred, let me sow love.
> Where there is injury, pardon.
> Where there is discord, union.
> Where there is doubt, faith.
> Where there is despair, hope.
> Where there is darkness, light.
> Where there is sadness, joy.
>
> Grant that I may not so much seek to be
>   consoled as to console,
> To be understood as to understand,
> To be loved as to love.
> For it is in giving that I receive.
> It is in pardoning that I am pardoned.
> And it is in dying that I am born to eternal life.[1]

In the first stanza we see the request to bring faith, hope, and love to others. The second provides the means for our doing this, through giving up the demands of our egos. The prayer is to love, not to be loved, and to console, not to be consoled. This is the opposite of our desire to be loved and taken care of by others.

The last line provides the foundation upon which the

structure is built. I am reminded of a song written by Bob Dylan and immortalized by Jimi Hendrix called "All Along the Watchtower." If you listen to it carefully, you will hear that it is written backwards. The dialogue is from characters who speak in the first stanza, but the scene is set for their approach in the last stanza.

The interesting thing about the Peace Prayer of Saint Francis is that, in a sense, it is also written backwards. The bedrock upon which it rests is the experience of dying to the self and being born again. When we "die to self," we are able to love rather than to seek love, and to console rather than to be consoled. And it is in loving and consoling that we are able to become instruments of healing and peace.

As we move about in our various social worlds, it will be through dying to our concern for the self and focusing our concern upon God that we will manifest a changed heart. It is a process that works from the inside out. As we move about in the outside we will see that a concern for others involves our experiencing a deeper love for them. This love in many instances involves a true dying to the self, for the self will always find reasons not to love someone.

If we return to our story one more time, we can see how this works. What if the stranger had said at the beginning, "You will be given the ability to grant peace to people, but only to those whom you feel are worthy." Now this seemingly slight difference would yield interesting consequences. Chances are that as we moved through our lives we would become choosy about who would receive peace. At first we might be fairly open, but soon we would be looking for people to earn our gift. In essence, we would look for people who would pander to the needs of our egos. They would have to be complimenting us, attending to our needs, or otherwise helping us along in some way. We would end up with a quid pro quo with respect to the granting of peace. In the end, we really wouldn't be acting much differently from the way we act now. We would be trying to give good feelings to those who are good to us and would be unwilling to grant peace to others.

One issue that this raises is worth discussing at some length. This concerns how to deal with evil. Specifically, how can we deal effectively yet lovingly and peacefully with people who are overtly evil? These are the people who are so involved with their own ego needs that they will stop at nothing to satisfy them. We see this evil writ large in repressive regimes such as Nazi Germany, Stalinist Russia, and certain dictatorships today. But we are likely to run into this problem in our daily lives as well. Whatever organization or institution you are associated with is likely to have its share of people who are so given over to self-gratification that it characterizes their very existence. This is of great concern to those of us trying to follow Christ. What happens when someone who is trying to die to self runs into someone who is consumed by ego needs? Will the person dying to self be "run over" by the other? Won't this naturally happen, since the follower of Christ will be more concerned with spreading love than stopping evil?

Since most of us are not directly involved in the battle against repressive political regimes, we can focus on the day-to-day evil that we are likely to face. To begin with, it is in sin, in the turning away from God, that people seek to harm others so that they can gratify their own ego needs. Again, consider the passage from the fifth chapter of Galatians, which says that giving oneself over to self-indulgence leads to a host of improper and damaging actions. Saint Paul concludes this list of actions by saying, "I am warning you, as I warned you before: those who do such things will not inherit the kingdom of God" (5:21).

Self-indulgent people will be quick to anger, extremely self-serving, or given to sexual immorality and jealousy. How do we deal with such people and with the situations they create? The following four-step process is helpful in deciding what to do.

1. *Determine the physical or emotional threat involved.*

You will need to take immediate action if physical or emotional abuse is involved. You should seek help as soon as possible. Find the best means of getting protection, and look for assistance from support groups and others.

2. *Ask whether you have faced this type of difficulty before.*

In a less threatening situation, it is helpful to do some internal and external assessment. This is important, for while you may not be in a state of crisis, as you would be if there were direct abuse involved, the daily grind of being around someone whom you feel exhibits one or more of the behaviors that Saint Paul mentions above can be very debilitating.

One worthwhile question to ask is whether a similar issue has come up in your past. It may be something in your own psychological makeup that is causing the problem. I will use myself as an example here. I discovered after some time that I had a problem with authority figures. It seemed that whoever I worked for was someone I quickly came to criticize and condemn. I would even go so far as to say that I would call them "evil." After a while, however, I started to realize that the problem wasn't so much with them as with me. I found that I really am a very independent person who resents having to work for other people.

Once I realized this, I was able to make some adjustments. Since I work in organizations with clear lines of authority, and I am not in a financial position that allows me to leave, I know that I can't simply quit to pursue a life of total freedom. I have to get used to working for other people. Once I accepted this, I was able to deal with my situation in a much better way. I also learned to stop condemning people I worked for and to look for their positive traits. In many instances, I have come to see them as similar to me. That is, I see them as people who are struggling to get through life and get their jobs done. It wasn't until I realized that the same issue was coming up in my life again and again, however, that I came to this understanding.

3. *Determine a course of action.*

After honestly appraising whether the problem is yours or theirs, and having determined that, indeed, someone else is the problem, the time comes to decide what to do about it. One key is determining whether the situation can be confronted directly or requires some other means. A social science book titled *Exit, Voice, and Loyalty*² sums up the alternatives. One can either leave, express displeasure, or stay and just be quiet. Even from a Christian perspective, there is no one way that will fit in all situations. If the situation is grievous enough, and you determine that there is really nothing you can do about it, then leaving might be your best option. If there is something you can do about it, then speaking out might be the best. If it really isn't a serious matter, and it is not something you want to disassociate from an organization about, then loyalty might be the answer.

4. *Maintain a sense of peace while acting.*

One of the most heart-wrenching aspects of dealing with the behaviors Saint Paul mentions is what it does to us as individuals. The behaviors have a tendency either to depress us or to make us angry and querulous ourselves. I have seen countless people consumed by hatred and anger as a result of dealing with a difficult situation. Preventing this requires a constant connection with God, as well as an honest appraisal of what your course of action will do to you emotionally. Make sure that you maintain a sense of peace throughout most of what you undertake. If you feel you are going to have difficulty, seek the advice and counsel of friends, and build time into your day to find a source of strength and peace through communion with God.

Remember, too, that the world is always going to be an imperfect place. We will never see situations resolved to our total satisfaction. I know someone, for example, who is constantly lamenting that in spite of an excellent education and superb credentials she is unable to keep a job for very long, much less to advance. She keeps running into people who block her advancement. As a result, she either complains to such a great extent that she gets fired, or she ends up leaving of her own accord. She often describes the people who get in her way as "evil" or "untrustworthy." What she is ignoring is that the world wasn't set up for our well-being. There simply are difficulties that we must face. Hoping for perfection flies in the face of reality. So when facing people exhibiting the "works of the flesh" that Saint Paul mentions, do not unrealistically think that everything will eventually work out perfectly. The trick is to deal with the situation as best you can, to change what you can, but not to become despondent if the problem persists. There will always be imperfect and evil actions. There will also always be the peace of God, however.

Hopefully, taking these steps will help in dealing with evil. The main thing to remember is that an honest attempt to change your heart does not mean that you have to give in to everyone. Remember that Jesus himself faced evil in a forthright manner. He threw the moneychangers out of the Temple and ordered Satan away when he was tempted. Remember also that Jesus did not let evil deter him from his mission, and that this mission was one of love.

Our "outside" lives are always going to contain difficulties. Though we have strong convictions and desires to do what is right, we may feel pulled to act in other ways. The "outside" life is the place where we mess it up, where we want to foster love but get caught up in our own desires and emotions and find ourselves doing exactly the opposite. Thus we can easily become despondent and ashamed of our own actions. But God loves us no matter what, and God's son sent a comforter to us in the Holy Spirit. In this we can experience forgiveness, peace, joy, and a place of new beginnings. Here our unworthiness is erased and our outer life can become in some manner a reflection of divine love. This is what it means to act with a Christ-centered heart.

The Journey: The Outward Journey

Carry around with you throughout the day some reminder of Christ. This might be a cross, a rosary, a nail, or anything at all that will remind you of Christ's love and sacrifice for you. Touch this object throughout the day, especially when you feel stressed or when you feel you may not be reacting to something in the way you would like to. Feel Christ's presence with this touch, and act accordingly.

EIGHT

Prayer: Thoughts from the Desert

Prayer is a singularly unique experience. It encompasses so many things, yet it is really one thing. It is, quite simply, ourselves before God. Within that simple statement, however, are a host of human actions and emotions. This, more than anything else, is the realm of the changed heart. Prayer is where we look at our lives, at our attempts to live according to the gospels, and find the shortcomings of our existence. Here we find the sorrows of life, the sorrows we are responsible for, as well as the joys of experiencing God within this life. Here, too, we may look at our interactions with others and find the space to examine them from a larger perspective. We may look at the desire for sanctification versus the desire for the pleasures of the world and find

101

out which desire is leading the way for us. Prayer provides, and often demands, opportunities for an appraisal of our selfish interests against our higher concerns.

All of this indicates that prayer itself is a transformative process. It is no less than opening to God while also examining our personal conduct to see the evidence of this opening.

Several hundred years ago a monk in the desert named Nilus wrote ten statements about prayer. I don't know much about him, other than that he was among the Desert Fathers who, in the early years of Christianity, chose to retreat into the desert of present-day Egypt in order to leave the world and be with God. Nilus occupies a rather small place in Benedicta Ward's *Sayings of the Desert Fathers*. His ten statements are all that there is from him. Perhaps that is all that is known of him.

So here I offer you ten statements from a monk of many centuries ago, an obscure figure who nonetheless wrote some powerful and interesting statements that get to the heart of so much of what I have written thus far. Most of these statements pertain to prayer, to that unique place of the self before God.[1]

1. *Everything you do in revenge against a brother who has harmed you will come back to your mind at the time of prayer.*

I have come to notice something very unusual of late. It is the number of times that people (including myself) criticize others when they are not around. I first noticed this about the obvious targets. These are the people who are somewhat odd or have unusual mannerisms or characteristics. But I have also noticed that anyone is fair game. Every person can be criticized for something. Some aspect of their personality can be exaggerated and criticized, some element of their lives can be enlarged and made fun of. The problem is, in walking away from a group engaging in such an activity, you have to wonder what they are saying about you. And don't think that people aren't talking about you! I mention this because gossip is the most frequent way that people are harmed these days, and often idle talk has a vengeful quality about it.

We criticize those whom we feel are speaking ill of us. You might think that this is fairly innocuous behavior. After all, everyone else is doing it. However, it can come to be the distinguishing mark of your personality. I know people who can't get through a meeting without criticizing someone else for being stupid, lazy, or incompetent. It seems as if there is always someone out there who simply doesn't have the knowledge or the common sense to do her or his job, and this has to be pointed out. Of course, this makes the person doing the criticizing appear to be superior—which may be the reason for their behavior. Still, you have to wonder if all that negativity is worth it.

Another side effect of criticizing others points more directly to Father Nilus's statement. You have to wonder what such criticism does to the one doing the criticizing. Does it harden him or her to the faults of others? It certainly does obstruct one from loving the person being criticized. How can you commit character assassination one moment and practice ways of loving that person the next?

When we pray, thoughts such as these may come to haunt us—and if they don't, they certainly should! What we have done to harm our brothers and sisters will stand between us and God. Remember, after all, that we are called to love God *and* our neighbor. Harming those around us in the end only harms us, because it gets in the way of our experiencing the love of God in a more complete sense.

2. *Prayer is the seed of gentleness and the absence of anger.*

We live in angry times. As I write this, the country is embroiled over the question of whether President Clinton had an affair with a young woman, and whether he asked her to commit perjury in testimony concerning her relations with him. This is an emotional story, and people are prone to get angry one way or another. The media don't really help matters much. Morning, noon, and night, people on television are speaking to one another in anger, making accusations and counteraccusations about this issue.

Can you imagine coming to prayer with such an attitude? Can you imagine fanning your anger and bitterness over an issue until you are aflame with emotion? This is not to say that one shouldn't speak openly and honestly to God about a disappointment. Still, at some point, prayer has to be about opening yourself to the love of God, about experiencing God's peace. Within this peace is that "seed of gentleness" that Nilus mentions. It is a seed that, planted in prayer, can be nourished in our daily interactions with others. It can lead to a peaceful approach to life and to those around us. What a blessing to take prayer beyond your allotted prayer time and to embody this seed of gentleness and absence of anger in your walk through life.

3. *Prayer is a remedy against grief and depression.*

Physician and author Larry Dossey spends a good deal of time looking at the medical benefits of prayer.[2] He cites formal experiments—complete with control groups and statistical analyses—showing that being prayed for does actually help patients in hospital settings. These, I think, are important studies, and I encourage anyone interested in the topic to take a look at his books.

Grief and depression, two psychological conditions, are medical conditions as well, inasmuch as they involve the body in a variety of ways. Depression in particular is often referred to as a clinical condition. Sadly, it is also a condition that is becoming more prevalent among the population.

Can prayer help both depression and grief? It would be interesting to conduct an empirical study to see if it really does. The anecdotal evidence I have witnessed is compelling. I have seen prayer uphold a family torn by the loss of a child. I have seen prayer sustain a family through marital difficulties. I, myself, have been upheld by prayer when I was emotionally wrecked by some event.

Prayer is a powerful remedy for grief and depression. It opens the heart to God and to the loving kindness found therein. It sustains.

4. *Go, sell all that belongs to you and give it to the poor and taking up the cross, deny yourself; in this way you will be able to pray without distraction.*

This is the most difficult and extreme of Father Nilus's pronouncements. Recently, I read this admonition to a group I was leading in the study of spirituality and everyday life, asking how we might apply it to our lives, and expecting a fairly abstract discussion.

"You just do it," said one man, who happened to be a priest.

I was taken aback. Many of us have heard or read various interpretations of this admonition. It was, of course, what Jesus told the rich young man when he kept asking Jesus how to inherit the kingdom of God. Most of us immediately want to jump to some way of dealing with this statement that gets us off the hook. "Surely this statement doesn't apply to me. Jesus just meant this to apply to the rich young man—this was just what *he* needed to do to attain the kingdom of heaven." Or perhaps Jesus was using hyperbole. Maybe he just meant that we shouldn't hold on to our possessions too tightly, that we should give a little bit to the poor and not agonize over it.

But what about just doing it? This, of course, is not something that most of us can do in good conscience. Those of us with children rightly feel obligations to them.

Is there some way, though, that tying this sentiment to prayer life is helpful? I think it is a way of bringing out more profoundly the softer interpretations of Jesus' advice, that is, those interpretations that say that we can get something out of Jesus' pronouncements without a strict, literal interpretation. I think a strong desire for some material possession or for some higher position will get in the way of prayer life. Conversely, a more detached attitude toward one's possessions and social standing will yield a deeper prayer life. It might even be true that the less one holds on, the less one tries to manipulate the environment to get what one needs, the deeper one's prayer life becomes. It's certainly worth a try.

5. *Whatever you have endured out of love of wisdom will bear fruit for you at the time of prayer.*

I have become intrigued lately with the whole notion of "losing it." It seems to happen all the time, if I take the words of the people around me seriously. People lose it when things don't go their way, when decisions are made that aren't consistent with their interests. People also lose it when they have to deal with others who exasperate them or have differing views of the world. What happens when people lose it is that they let off quite a bit of emotional steam. They become agitated, stomp around, curse, and so on. At the end of this they go home fatigued and angry. I know something about this because I have been there myself.

I am equally intrigued with another concept. I recently attended a lay conference in which the idea of being "transparent to Christ" was mentioned quite a bit. I've occasionally heard it mentioned since then as well. What does this mean, being transparent to Christ? I think it means being transparent to those around you. It means that you don't have secret agendas, that you don't live mainly for this world. You can be seen through by those around you. When they look at you, they see the love of Christ. In my mind I see transparency as being similar to light, that is, in seeing you, people can see through you to the light of Christ. As Saint Paul says in Ephesians, "For once you were darkness, but now in the Lord you are light. Live as children of light" (5:8).

Perhaps becoming transparent to Christ is one way to keep from losing it. It allows you to become less concerned with everyone else's agenda. Perhaps, too, this is similar to Nilus's statement. It is in becoming transparent to Christ that we become lovers of wisdom. This enables us to endure life's events more calmly. This, in turn, bears fruit when we open ourselves to God in prayer.

6. *If you want to pray properly, do not let yourself be upset or you will run in vain.*

Several years ago I had a disturbing and profound dream. It was a time of turmoil in my life. I was finishing up my doctoral dissertation and really having a rough go of it. My dissertation adviser took a grant to study on the other side of the continent and thus was not around to give advice. It also seemed that he was distancing himself from his students. For my part, I had chosen a topic that raised some particularly difficult research and writing issues. In hindsight, I probably should not have been writing on that topic at all. In any event, I'd wanted to get the thing over and done with so that I could get on with my life, which at that time meant getting my degree and becoming a teacher.

When I thought that the dissertation was finished, I took it before my adviser (who had flown in for a few days) and my readers, thinking that the work would be approved and that I would be on my way to a teaching post. Instead, my readers decided I needed to undertake what turned out to be two more years of revisions. During that time the academic job market continued to decline, and my adviser, who had once been enthusiastic toward my work, was now not even lukewarm toward my abilities and did not foresee my getting a job in academics. Although I managed to finish my degree, I was crushed. I was angry at the university, angry with my adviser, and bitter about the whole academic system.

Then I had a dream. I dreamed that I was at a convention in my discipline (political science) being held at a large hotel in Chicago, on the shores of Lake Michigan. I was walking around a room that was packed with people, having the feeling that this would be the last time I would be at such a convention. I was feeling very angry about this. Then I saw my adviser sitting at the head of a table (as he always did when he was teaching a class). One of my fellow graduate students was standing next to me, and we were looking over at my adviser. My friend said that I really should hate this man. I had a quite different feeling. I felt I needed to forgive him.

Soon it seemed that this was all too much, so I walked out of the hotel. I looked back and saw the hotel separate from the land and go floating out into Lake Michigan, leaving me behind. I wandered about the city with a general feeling of being lost.

Looking at the dream, it both accurately and symbolically showed that I *was* being left behind. The discipline went on while I ended up working in other areas. I could easily become consumed with anger toward the academic system and toward my adviser. What would be the point, though? Would I not just be upset all the time, and would I not, as Nilus says, run in vain? And what about my prayer life? Is it possible to pray honestly and openly without somehow getting to the spirit of forgiveness?

7. *Do not be always wanting everything to turn out as you think it should, but rather as God pleases, then you will be undisturbed and thankful in your prayer.*

I'm sure that you have had several opportunities to reflect upon how things have gone in your life. I usually do this at the end of the year or around the time of my birthday. I often find that things didn't turn out exactly as I would have liked. In fact, much of my life has been a series of unexpected events. If ten years ago someone would have said I would be in the place I am now, I would have thought it highly unlikely. Life depends so much upon outside arbitrary and capricious events and people. Thinking things will always turn out as we expect is often an exercise in futility.

Here is an example of what I mean. Sam was working for a company, trying to get settled into a particular position. Try as he might, however, he simply couldn't get along with his boss. As a result, he transferred to another area. In this area he had exposure to the very top levels of the organization. At first, this position seemed as if it were filled with opportunity. Sam resolved to work hard and make a good impression. One of the executives with whom he worked, however, just didn't like him at all, but it was a very unusual situation. It seemed that the executive was really tolerant of incompetence as long as it came from someone he liked. Toward others, and toward Sam in particular, he was highly intolerant. When Sam grew frustrated at this situation and eased up a bit, the executive was quick to point out to him and to others that he appeared to lack motivation.

Sam felt he was getting nowhere. Then through an unusual and rapid turn of events, the executive left the company. He was replaced by another executive, this time someone who really liked Sam and saw him as someone with a lot of potential. He even promoted Sam into another position.

The point of this story is that life has a strong capricious element to it. For Sam had not changed anything about himself—not his appearance, his work habits, or his views. But because someone else took over, his professional life took a dramatic turn for the better.

This illustration helps us to get at Nilus's statement. If we are always expecting things to turn out the way we would like, we are in for some big surprises. Our prayer life is likely to be one of unending frustration. If we realize the capriciousness of life, yet decide to worship God in all circumstances, then our prayer life is more likely to be peaceful and undisturbed.

8. *Happy is the monk who thinks he is the outcast of all.*

It is amazing sometimes to think about the lengths to which people will go to get a sense of belonging. This was particularly true for me when I was younger. Like most teenagers, I struggled with the sense of not really fitting in, and I really wanted to be seen as part of the "in crowd." The harder I tried, however, the more foolish I seemed.

I am reminded of something I read recently in Kathleen Norris's book about Benedictine spirituality, *The Cloister Walk*. In this book, which recounts her experiences as an oblate Benedictine, she refers to her own spiritual development, saying that she finally came to accept "the cross of myself, a burden I've carried ever since childhood, and felt so acutely in my teens."[3]

This simple statement says so much. For one, it indicates that in many respects the selves we carry around are actually crosses. Here I am thinking of the ego needs we have. I, for example, tend to be a fairly sensitive person who can be hurt by what I perceive as the cruelty of others. I carry this cross around, at times allowing it to dictate how I feel and what I think about others. And it's true that I was acutely aware of this cross in my teens.

Oddly enough, recognizing my cross has liberated me from it. Once I saw my character flaw—or more charitably put, my particular psychological makeup—for what it is, its hold upon me dissipated. This was an extremely pleasurable feeling, as if a weight were being lifted from me. I see, then, the sense of saying that a monk who is an outcast is happy. I would say it this way: Happy is the person who recognizes their particular need to belong and is able to let go of it.

9. *The monk who loves interior peace will remain invulnerable to the shafts of the enemy, but he who mixes with crowds constantly receives blows.*

Mihaly Csikszentmihalyi in his recent book *Finding Flow* writes about the importance of balancing time alone and time with other people. According to his research, "In our society, the average person spends about one-third of his or her waking time alone. Persons who spend much more or much less time by themselves often have problems."[4] Csikszentmihalyi finds that creative, happy people tend to find a good balance between being introverts and extroverts. They know how to be alone, but they also know how to be with people.

Being a monk, of course, Nilus upholds the idea of solitude. I think there is a way of taking his sentiment, however, and mixing it with Csikszentmihalyi's findings. The trick is to take a sense of interior peace into all of your interactions. This is a way of blending prayer life with real life. Prayer life can be a way of finding peace through God. It can also grant a sense of peace so that while you move about in crowds, the blows of life are softened, or perhaps not even felt at all.

10. *The servant who neglects his master's work should expect a beating.*

It's hard to look at this last statement without laughing. There is a way of looking at it somewhat seriously, though. If we look at ourselves as God's servants (as we are), then an interesting view emerges. If we neglect our Master's work, then we *should* expect a beating. That is, we will suffer from the assaults of the world much more acutely than would otherwise be the case. We will have nothing to shield us from the difficulties that we face. We will not have the benefit of that calm described in Psalm 23. We will be totally at the will of the outside world. We will experience a beating.

I've heard it said that a person who relies upon the external world to provide highs and lows is going to be jerked around a lot. Many of us quite naturally and unconsciously live according to the external world. We feel good when circumstances are favorable for us, and bad when they aren't. Even as uncontrollable an event as rain has a way of bringing us down.

Prayer is a way of protecting us against feeling jerked around. It opens up the heart and soul and reminds us of the rock we have to lean upon. This, more than anything, is the message of an obscure monk from a distant century.

The Journey: Prayer

Stop now and spend five minutes praying. Begin with experiencing the love of God. Then express to God your deepest concerns and your worst shortcomings. Ask God for assistance with these. Next, thank God for the blessings of your life. Finally, open your heart to God and experience a love that transcends all the boundaries of time and space.

NINE

A Wise Heart

Recently, I experienced a week of death. My son's first-base coach in Little League died in a tragic automobile accident. He was a young man, still in his thirties, with a young son. The next day my mother's best friend died of cancer. On that same day my wife attended the funeral of an old high school friend who also died of cancer.

The following day I ran into a friend of mine at work who was uncharacteristically wearing a tie on a designated casual day. I asked him why he was so dressed up.

"I have to go to a funeral," he said. "A friend of mine, the tennis coach at my kids' school, died."

"Heart attack?" I asked.

"Yeah."

Having passed the age of forty and moved officially into middle age, I do not take such weeks lightly. They are reminders that this life does not go on forever. This is something that is hard to put into words, but I certainly experience it from time to time. There is nothing quite like looking over a baseball field and expecting to see a familiar face, only to realize that you will never see that face again.

What does this have to do with the experience of a centered heart? Everything in the world. It is important to realize that a centered heart does not indicate a static experience. As already noted in previous chapters, we live in a world full of change. Just when you think you have things figured out, just when you feel you have found your spiritual center, something unexpected happens. Death, of course, is the ultimate unexpected event.

One proverb is helpful in thinking about the difficulties of life. "Wisdom is at home in the mind of one who has understanding, but it is not known in the hearts of fools" (Proverbs 14:33). Wisdom, not being known in the hearts of fools, must be something in the very hearts of those who have understanding. We have talked a great deal about a centered heart's being a loving heart. A heart centered upon Christ is also one possessing wisdom.

Wisdom is the final way in which we will look at the centered heart as it relates to the interaction of the self with life. Like so much else written about in this book, it has an internal and external quality. It is something that is experienced from within, but only in respect to the external events of life. As we will see, wisdom is best understood in relation to a centered heart, rather than as something independent from it. In other words, it is best to experience Christ first and then to experience wisdom, rather than to seek wisdom in and of itself.

Let's begin by understanding something about how

experiencing wisdom helps. To do this, we'll look at the events mentioned earlier in this chapter. A week in which several acquaintances die is certainly reason for anyone to pause. In thinking about death, one can discern in it the opening of the door for a return to a loving God. So much is written about this, as both standard theology and popular accounts of near-death experiences, that I will not dwell on this point. Suffice it to say that a Christ-centered life provides the means of experiencing love even when faced with the finality of death.

Death also speaks directly to loving your neighbor. Death, quite simply, is the end of our existence on this earth. The above notwithstanding, all of the reasoning and comforting in the world cannot take away the pain felt upon experiencing the death of a loved one. Death presents us with the opportunity to feel compassion for others. Human beings are, after all, fragile creatures who will experience the pain of their own death and who must learn to live with the death of those close to them. From the richest of the rich to the poorest of the poor, we will all suffer from death, and we all need compassion to deal with this suffering.

Spiritual wisdom not only allows for such "logical" understandings to take place, I believe that it also opens our eyes to grace. This is more of an experiencing than an intellectual comprehension. Here is an example of what I mean. The week in which I was barraged with death, I had the opportunity of taking the Eucharist at a church close to where I work. The church celebrates the Eucharist every day at noon, and I try to go at least once a week. What makes this celebration special is that it takes place not in the large sanctuary, but in a small chapel to the side of the sanctuary. The chapel provides a more intimate setting.

As I sat in this chapel, getting ready for the ceremony, I looked about at the small number of people around me. One or two were people whom I knew. A few others were people whom I see downtown from time to time but don't really know that well. The remaining number were complete strangers. It occurred to me that this might be something like a celebration in heaven. Here we were, a group of people, some known and some unknown to one another, gathered together out of the love of Christ. Something about this love surrounded me, and I felt as if I had had a foretaste of a celebration in heaven. This, I know, was a grace, a mercy, an experience of wisdom that came from even as meager and incomplete an understanding of God as mine.

Life, as we know, is filled with tragedies and heartaches requiring spiritual, heartfelt wisdom. As human beings, we walk around with disappointments. We feel the sting of broken hearts and shattered dreams. The world, in some way, hasn't provided just the thing we need. There is, in a sense, a rational basis for this. You and I are imperfect people living among other imperfect people in an imperfect world. This situation is ripe for things not quite working out for us.

Wisdom in this setting is to be able to see the Christ in what is happening around us. This does not necessarily mean, as so many seem to think, that God creates bad events in our lives so that God's will may be worked out in a particular way. This is what people are saying when something bad happens and they say that it is God's will. So when a particular job doesn't come along or a loved one dies at a young age, people who think along these lines will say that it is God's will.

Now it's not that I am adamantly opposed to this viewpoint. I think, however, that it tends to look at things from the wrong perspective. The belief that God is arranging the particulars of my life in a certain way so that I might grow in a particular manner places me far more at the center of things than I am comfortable with. It may be that God does so arrange the details of people's lives (I don't know). The important point, though, is that regardless of what happens in my life, I need to find ways of loving, honoring, and serving God. God is at the center, not me. Even my spiritual development, while important, is not the chief end of life. That place belongs to God.

Passing a difficult situation off as God's will may not be at the heart of wisdom. What is available is for us to reflect upon such a situation to see how we can grow toward becoming better servants of God. This fits with David Nicholl's sentiment in *Holiness* that suffering is the best teacher of compassion and joy (the "loving your neighbor" side of things). Contrary to the way we ordinarily look at life, Nicholl says that the worst thing that could happen to us is that we should be cut off from suffering. To have perfect health, interesting work, plenty of money, and no experience with suffering, he argues, would turn a person "into a monster, something unnatural, incapable of compassion for other creatures." Nicholl argues that to be cut off from suffering "is automatically to be cut off from joy." This, I am assuming, is the joy of compassion. Nicholl concludes by saying that whenever we are removed from suffering for any length of time, "we can be certain that we are on the wrong path."[1]

A wise heart will find, even within suffering, the blessings of God. It might even be true that a wise heart will find the blessings of God *especially* within suffering. It has been true for me that even during my darkest hours, when I was emotionally devastated, people around me have supported and uplifted me. This blessing was what allowed me to survive. There were also healing words from the Scriptures and moments during worship services that sustained me during such times. Were I wiser, I would probably recognize more of God's blessings during the difficulties of my life. And the result of suffering has been a growing sense of compassion for others. It is not that I seek out such suffering (I do not) but that often the result of suffering is, in fact, the realization that others suffer too.

Is there some way of improving wisdom so that one becomes "wise" in a greater number of life's situations? Again, I believe this desire has things the wrong way around. Wisdom is simply a quality of one who has placed her or his faith and trust in Jesus. It doesn't require a course, which would probably be counterproductive anyway.

Some thoughts from the twentieth-century monk Thomas Merton are illuminating. In his book *The Silent Life,* Merton writes about the important elements of monasticism. He begins by writing, "A monk is a man who has been called by the Holy Spirit to relinquish the cares, desires and ambitions of other men, and devote his entire life to seeking God." The odd thing, as Merton points out, is that no one on earth knows what it means to seek God until that person has been found by God. "In the end," Merton says, "no one can seek God unless he has already begun to find Him. No one can find God without having first been found by Him. A monk is a man who seeks God because he has been found by God."[2]

The argument easily applies outside of the monastic world. A person on a spiritual path is not someone who is really looking for God. God has already found that person, has already ignited within him or her a longing for the eternal Presence. Those seeking to live a Christ-centered life need not despair of being outside God's presence. Like the monk, that person is already "a man [person] of God."[3]

Enhancing wisdom, then, is not really the primary concern of the Christian. The real issue is to live as one who has been found by God. Such a life contains within it the quality of wisdom, just as it contains the qualities associated with the fruits of the Spirit (love, joy, self-control, and so forth). The primary process is in finding ways to place Christ at the center of one's life, and not with finding ways to increase wisdom.

If a changed heart is a wiser one, then does that not mean that the decisions of a spiritual person are some-

how better? Will I be able to make the best career decisions, for example, or make decisions that will always
benefit my family physically, economically, and socially?
Isn't that what is meant by wisdom?

Let's sharpen such questions a little more by looking
at a concrete example. I am currently involved in selling
my home. This is not the result of the robbery I mentioned earlier in this book. It is simply the case that we
have outgrown our home. Now, how is spiritual wisdom going to help me here? Will it help me to sell my
house at just the right price, at just the right time to just
the right people (whoever they may be)? In buying a
house, will it help me to find a house that is reasonably
priced and free of defect?

There is a sense in which wisdom helps in something
as worldly as selling a house. However, this mundane
wisdom is really secondary to a spiritual one. Wisdom
in a spiritual sense, for me, means understanding that no
matter what happens, God still loves me. So if I make a
mistake by selling the house at too low a price, I still
have the love of God, no matter what others around me
might say. Additionally, I know that other things are more
important than the sale of the current house or the pur-
chase of the next. My standing before God is much more
important. Spiritual wisdom releases me from the tyr-
anny of thinking that selling my house is the most important thing in my life.

This perspective does filter down to the practical experiences I will have in selling my house. With Christ at
the center of my heart, I am open to whatever the Spirit

may reveal to me as I go through this experience. Perhaps it will bring people into my life in need of special attention. Spiritual wisdom opens me up to new, unforeseen possibilities. This is far more important (and realistic) than expecting discernment to give me some special knowledge that will allow me to sell my house at top dollar.

The centered heart points the way to a wiser, saner way of living. That, I think, is what the proverb means in saying, "Wisdom is at home in the mind who has understanding." This is also behind Saint Paul's sentiments in the following verses:

> And this is my prayer, that your love may overflow more and more with knowledge and full insight to help you to determine what is best, so that in the day of Christ you may be pure and blameless, having produced the harvest of righteousness that comes through Jesus Christ for the glory and praise of God (Philippians 1:9–11).

It is the focus of wisdom (here phrased as knowledge and insight) that is important. To improve in purity, righteousness, and love is really a better goal than improving one's material surroundings.

Wisdom, which does involve in a deep sense the relation of the self with the world, is closely aligned with being able to experience God in the moment. It is, in fact, through understanding God in the moment that we find purity, righteousness, and love. This sentiment is consistent with those of Celtic spirituality, which is growing in popularity of late. One Celtic prayer says this:

Christ be with me sleeping hours,
And Christ be with me waking,
Through all watches aiding powers,
Christ with me undertaking,
No day nor any night without him,
Nor any night without him.
God be with me to protect,
The Spirit there to strengthen,
Lord be with me to direct
As span of life doth lengthen.[4]

Such sentiments cause Esther de Waal to write that from the Celts comes "this vivid sense of a God who knows, loves, supports, is close at hand, and actually present in their [the Celts] lives. Of course this sense of divine presence and protection are found elsewhere in the history of the Church, but I feel that nowhere else is it found with quite the same intensity. It is one of the many gifts of the Celtic tradition to us, and it is perhaps the most important."[5] This sense of the presence of God is strongly linked to a Christ-centered life. Wisdom is among the many gifts that this presence provides.

We should examine one final aspect of wisdom. I recently attended a conference on spirituality in the workplace. The final evening of the workshop consisted of a panel discussion between the workshop participants and the program speakers. The discussion lasted almost two hours. Although the forum was planned to be an open-ended one capable of dealing with several issues, it didn't turn out that way. One middle-aged woman stood up and asked about having the wisdom to discern her vocation. In other words, how does one know what God wants you to do? How do you know if you are doing it? When thinking about making a career change, how do you get to what, exactly, God desires for you?

Vocational wisdom is a pressing concern for many. Based upon the admittedly small sample of people at this conference, it is on a lot of people's minds, and not only on those of the young. Interestingly, no single answer emerged from this panel or from the audience itself. Some people recounted specific instances when God almost *told* them what to do. Others referred to the Scripture where people (Moses, Saint Paul, Jonah, and so on) were told what to do quite clearly and were kept on that path almost against their will at times. Still others talked of their own struggles over a lifetime of trying to understand what God expected of them vocationally.

Two issues are evident. One is that our culture's focus upon success colors our understanding of what God might want of us. Because we may not be wildly successful according to the values of Western culture (few people are), then we *must* be on the wrong path. God surely intends more for me than this. If I were on the right path, I would be making more money, or at least having more of an impact on those around me. The community would view me as a success and uphold me as an example, someone to imitate.

This outlook flies in the face of historical Christianity. Was Saint Peter, who was supposedly crucified upside down, a great success by the world's standards? A lot of good Christians also died in Nazi concentration camps (along with a great many more good Jews). These are just two of several historical examples that could be cited to show that a solid belief in Christ or God doesn't necessarily lead to anything near success in this world. Shouldn't spiritual wisdom help in these sorts of situations? Wouldn't it have helped Saint Peter find a way to avoid violent death, and the good people persecuted in Germany from experiencing such horrid conditions?

The second issue is more mundane. Shouldn't wisdom provide at least some kind of indication as to which career path to take? Even if it is one that might lead to some suffering or personal deprivation (as exemplified by someone such as Mother Teresa) on my part, won't God at least tell me what it is I am supposed to do? Surely I wasn't meant to sit in this cubicle, work in this office, or pursue this boring career. What, however, am I *supposed* to do?

In my experience, very few people get clear indications about their vocation. It seems that most of us stumble along without any clear direction. We may see the importance of working with the poor, for example, but an opportunity for doing so that also allows us to support those who rely upon us financially never seems to present itself. Where is wisdom here?

The issues of our lack of "success," as well as the fact that most don't receive clear instructions about what to do next, are difficult ones with which to deal. Again, wisdom based upon a centered-heart experience is helpful in getting past these difficulties. A Christ-centered approach gets us to the understanding that no matter where we are, we are true failures as human beings, as well as true successes through Christ's redemption of us. With this experience, it is possible at long last to understand how material success may be separated from wisdom. Wisdom is more of an understanding of how to serve God, perhaps even if "only" in small ways, rather than an understanding of how one can benefit vocationally and materially. Put serving God first, and wisdom in the manner of better ways of service will develop.

This is even true of our second issue. Vocationally, the point is not whether you can decide with certainty where God wants you. It just seems to be the case that most people will never be given clear direction. Again, the issue is not so much whether you can find just the right spot. The concern is to serve God no matter where you are.

Having said that, I believe that some very interesting things can happen with a Christ-centered, service-oriented life. One aspect of wisdom of which anyone is readily capable is understanding one's gifts. Most people do some things very well, and these are also the things they enjoy doing. When they perform these activities, they enter a state of "flow," as described by researcher Mihaly Csikszentmihalyi. According to Csikszentmihalyi, flow is the state during which people experience a sense of effortless activity, in which they feel that their best skills are being used. The activities will be different for different people. "Athletes," as Csikszentmihalyi says, "refer to it [flow] as 'being in the zone,' religious mystics as being in 'ecstasy,' artists and musicians as aesthetic rapture. Athletes, mystics, and artists do very different things when they reach flow, yet their descriptions of the experience are remarkably similar."[6]

The initial vocation question indicates that people tend to discount their flow experiences because they feel they aren't ones that will necessarily result in wild material or even spiritual success. In other words, they keep looking for just the right situation and don't really pay attention to where their current skills are finding good use. Placing Christ at the center has a way of opening up the possibility for some practical wisdom. A Christ-centered life is one in which ways are found to love God and our neighbors no matter what occupation we may be pursuing. We don't have to go in search of the perfect occupation to have such "success" experiences.

A Christ-centered life actually frees us to enjoy our current work experiences, which just might lead to a deeper understanding of where we can find our truest joy. This may be either in our current job or in some future one. Once the pressure is off to find the ideal place, we can truly love and serve God where we are. Part of our service will include understanding our particular gifts and offering them to God and others no matter where we may happen to be sitting. This, I think, is a truer sense of wisdom than the myth that one can find just the right job at just the right time.

Since that workshop evening I have thought much about what I would say to the question posed about vocational wisdom. (Being an analytical type, I usually have to think things through before rendering anything like a respectable opinion.) With but a little time to speak, one would have to be very concise and succinct. I am tempted to return to the somewhat pithy, though hauntingly accurate, "Let go and let God." There is a sense in which abandonment to the service of God opens the door to a fulfilling life of love.

Wisdom, then, stands at an interesting place in our understanding of a Christ-centered existence. A Christ-centered life helps us to understand how to confront such hard issues as death with a heart that is concerned with loving God and loving our neighbors. Wisdom also forces us to realize that the drive for the perfect job pales in comparison to the spiritual drive to love and serve God in all things.

The Journey: Determine Your Gifts and Practice One

Ask some friends and loved ones what your gifts are, whether they be teaching, writing, interacting with others, counseling, or whatever. Add to this list of gifts any others that you feel you have. Pick one that is currently underutilized, but one that you would like to use more often. Think of some way that you can dedicate this gift to God's work, and spend a month practicing the gift both at work and in your spare time. Keep a journal of the events that take place as a result of this effort, and review it at the end of the month. Write a summary at the end of the month that includes any insights you received as a result of this exercise.

TEN

Living with Christ

As we come to the end of this book, two simple questions are worth discussing in slightly more detail. These questions have been in front of us all along, and we have answered them throughout. Yet the questions themselves are key. They get right down to the heart of the matter.

The two questions are the fundamental ones of *why* and *how*. Why should you live with Christ at the center of your heart? You are guaranteed neither riches nor fame with this approach. And if you decide to live in this manner in spite of the lack of guarantee, *how* do you do it? Does it involve some complex, mystical practice that takes years to refine?

Let's start with why and begin with a continuation of a familiar story. We all know the parable of the Prodigal Son, the story of a young man who leaves home to experience the pleasures of the world. Let's try setting the story in a modern context. Imagine a wealthy father who watches as the younger of his two sons goes off to pursue a life of debauchery. (If this sounds like a plot from a television series, forgive me). He stands by helpless as his son falls further and further into drinking, drugs, fornication—the whole mess. Finally, the father concludes that his son, whom he loves dearly, is hopeless. There is no way to get him to come back.

Understanding tough love, the father resigns himself to the fact that he can do nothing. When his son drops out of sight, he scans the paper daily, expecting him to turn up in the obituaries or in some crime report. Soon he gives up even on that. His son is gone. His therapist advises him to get on with his life. In spite of this, the father continues to love his son, wishing that he could do something.

The father's older son remains faithful. He does his chores, takes care of his share of the family business, and does the other things that faithful children do.

One day, after a long time has passed, the father and his remaining son are sitting outside on the porch, enjoying the sunset. Even with this, though, the father feels a degree of sadness. If only his younger son were here, then things would be complete.

Then, in the distance, a figure approaches. As the figure comes closer, it becomes apparent that it is a man. The father watches as the man comes closer. He starts to recognize the man but dares not get his hopes up too high. When the man is close enough, however, there is no denying it. This is the lost son.

The father jumps to his feet and runs to his son. He hugs him tightly, tears of joy streaming down the faces of both father and son. The father enthusiastically welcomes his son back into the family, throws a great party, and lets it be known that the returning son is to be showered with all that he can provide.

The older boy looks on in shock.

"Wasn't I always here for my father, through thick and thin?" he says to his wife.

"Wasn't I the one who took care of the family business when my father was so grief-stricken that he couldn't work?" he says to their accountant.

"Didn't I make sure that my mother was taken care of when she was sick?" he says to a family friend.

Unable to take it any longer, he confronts his father.

"Look," he says, "how can you treat my brother so kindly. Look at all the trouble he caused. I can see giving him something, but not so much. Surely he must pay for the pain he caused. I can't believe you think he should get what I get."

The father looks over at his son and sees the concern on his face. He tries to come up with a way to express the joy he feels, how retribution and anger can find no place within this joy.

"Your brother was lost, and now he is found" is all he can say.

What happens at this point, of course, is up to the participants. Illustrative for our purposes are the choices that *both* brothers now face. The older one can realize that there is a joy beyond simply being rewarded for good actions and punished for bad ones. In a sense, this is what this book is all about. Many times we feel that the world has been unjust to us. Like the older brother, we have done our duty. Still, someone or something has come along and harmed us. We are unable to get beyond our own self-centered interests.

What would have made the remaining son more apt to celebrate his brother's return? If anything, it would be having his heart centered upon the Christlike experience of love. This would have allowed him to labor not solely for things of this world but for the treasures of God's kingdom.

And what about the younger son? He is often forgotten when looking at the ending of the story. Yet he, too, has choices. He might expect to be continuously lavished with whatever riches the father has. What if these run out? To take something that might have come from the old series *Dallas,* what if the oil wells run dry? Does the younger son become consumed with anger?

There are even further questions once one takes the full spiritual significance of the Prodigal Son story into account. The father in the story is, of course, symbolic of God. In welcoming back the younger son, he is accepting him into the kingdom of God. Does the returning son understand what the riches of this kingdom are?

Spiritually speaking, it may well be that these riches are often misunderstood. Many of us came of age, after all, in a time when practices such as transcendental meditation were popular. As a former practitioner I really have nothing against it. However, what is interesting is all the medical data that was published concerning its benefits. It seems that other types of spiritually based practices also picked up the medical-benefit approach. Now we often see information about the benefits of meditation, yoga, tai chi, centering prayer, and so on. In a stress-filled society obsessed with the reduction of stress, the psychological/medical benefits of spiritual practices are often touted.

I have no doubts about the truth of the published studies. The problem is that we might easily place the cart before the horse regarding these accounts. As for the approach I have been talking about throughout this book, I do not offer it as a means to add a few years to your life or to bring down your blood pressure, though it may well do these things. Rather, I speak of a Christ-centered approach because it is an obligation we have as Christians. The fact that it is a *joyful* obligation, hence associated with happiness and perhaps even leading to health, is a secondary concern.

Let's return to the prodigal son to see how this might play out. The prodigal son of our times might come into the spiritual kingdom with certain expectations.

"Won't I be peaceful in all situations?" he might ask. "Won't my blood pressure go down and my cardiovascular system improve? Won't all of my decisions and opinions have the ring of truth to them?"

The fact is, leading a spiritual life is not necessarily going to make life any easier. Focusing on the potential by-products of such a life is really to lose perspective. Christ is the focus. Loving Christ in all things is the joy, not the physical or material things that might go along with this love.

A few years ago a man by the name of John Piper wrote a book that outlines a view similar to this, using the notion of a Christian hedonist (now there are two words you don't often see together!). *Desiring God: Meditations of a Christian Hedonist* begins with the intriguing view that the chief end of humankind is to glorify God by enjoying him forever.[1]

Enjoyment, with all its deeply felt satisfaction, is an integral part of Piper's Christian hedonism. It is something not to be pursued in and of itself but comes about by the glorification of God. Piper draws upon the Scriptures and such writers as C. S. Lewis to prove his point. Particularly compelling from the perspective of this book are the first three of his five convictions of Christian hedonism. These are:

1. The longing to be happy is a universal human experience, and it is good, not sinful.
2. We should never try to deny or resist our longing to be happy, as though it were a bad impulse. Instead we should seek to intensify this longing and nourish it with whatever will provide the deepest and most enduring satisfaction.
3. The deepest and most enduring happiness is found only in God.[2]

Piper's other two principles have to do with sharing the love of God and worshiping God.

This focus upon happiness really allows us to put together a final answer to the question of why you should lead a life centered upon God. The fact is that it is simply the way we are made. Our chief end, as it were, is to glorify God. Along with this glorification comes a depth of joy that is known in no other experience. So finding God's son in our hearts, we find a duty to glorify God in all things. Far from being onerous, this is a joyous duty. Living our lives in recognition of the Christ in our hearts is the fulfillment of this duty.

So much for the why. What about the how? To get at this question, let's look at a Greek word found in the Bible. *Agape* is a term that we understand as meaning "love." What many don't know is that agape is also associated with the Eucharist. In fact, the Eucharist was referred to as an agape, a "love-feast." Thus the *Oxford Companion to the Bible* talks of agape as the "common meal with which Christians first followed Christ's command at the last supper to 'do this in remembrance of me,' and later to 'feed my sheep.'" Interestingly, the *Oxford Companion to the Bible* also refers to 1 Corinthians 11:29 and 31 in saying that by eating in agape, "Christians will 'discern' Christ's presence in themselves and others together."[3]

Discerning Christ's presence in ourselves and others fits nicely with the theme of this book. Discerning his presence in us is simply finding him in our hearts. Discerning his presence in others is the ability to see Christ in the hearts of others. It is especially apt that the Eucharist, in all its mystery, somehow brings out this experience.

Focusing on the how of leading a Christ-centered life, I will use AGAPE as an acronym. Like the Eucharist, it is to bring about a discernment of the Christ in you and in others. It is part of creating the "love-feast" that a Christian's life can be. And AGAPE also has an element of prevention. It can prevent us from becoming like the prodigal son's older brother, that is, not apt to begrudge others their good fortune or to look at life as a system of rewards and punishments, but to experience the true grace of life.

At any rate, the AGAPE acronym is this:

Attention
Gratitude
Adventure
Presence
Exaltation

Let's look at each one of these in order. *Attention* is a key aspect of living a Christ-centered life. One thing I have discovered in my own experience, to use a metaphor that fits well with the biblical metaphors of gardening and bearing fruit, is that what you water, grows. In other words, the thoughts and feelings that you pay attention to (water) will grow. If you are angry about something and you think about it, it will grow. Conversely, if you are able to think about something else (something more peaceful or pleasant, for example) that thought or feeling will grow.

This simple "fact" often has far-reaching consequences. I've even read that something as simple as putting a rubber band around your wrist and popping it (hence causing a small amount of pain) when a negative thought enters your head can have a dramatic positive impact upon your thoughts, stopping you from watering the negative thought and allowing you to focus on more pleasurable experiences.

It might be helpful to ask yourself about your day-in, day-out negative thoughts. Try to find some method of not thinking these, and see how your experience may change.

Another way of dealing with life is through finding a way toward *gratitude* in all things. I recently talked to a young woman who goes so far as to keep a gratitude journal. Every morning she gets up and writes about what she is thankful for. Sometimes it's things that you might think she would be less than grateful about. For example, she writes about a particular physical ailment, seeing that it caused her to slow down and take a look at the fast pace with which she moves through life.

Another way to think about gratitude is to look at your life in perspective. Whenever I am particularly distressed, I recall an incident that took place about six years ago, something that could easily have cost my life. I was out burning some leaves and other assorted things when my shirt caught on fire. My children had recently been through a talk on the dangers of fire at their elementary school, and I had read in their materials about how you should "stop, drop, and roll" if you ever catch on fire. Even using this life-saving technique, however, I could not get the fire out. Finally, after a brief flare up into my face, I decided simply to rip the shirt off.

The result of this incident was a few nasty burns, which, luckily, healed completely. While I was healing, however, I happened to run into an acquaintance who is a paramedic. He noted the burns around my nose and said that if I had inhaled the flames, as I might well have done, I would most likely have burned my lungs. Infection would have set in, and I could easily have been dead a few days later.

Needless to say, the memory of this event makes me hug my wife and children a little harder and enjoy life a little more. It creates in me a grateful spirit.

The next word might seem out of place here. *Adventure* nonetheless has a place in the Christ-centered life. Perhaps a better phrase would be "positive adventure." Think about Saint Paul. Here is someone who made several extensive journeys throughout the known world. He suffered imprisonment, chastisement, and ridicule, as well as some undisclosed "thorn" in his side. Throughout all this, however, he was able to write of love and to look back upon his life and see that he had run a good race.

Now, granted, most of us don't lead the kind of life that Saint Paul did. Still, with the constant change most of us confront in modern life, adventure is not a word that is too far off the mark. Maintaining a Christ-centered heart within all the change will add a lot more peace and possibility to the adventure our lives will be. When in the midst of the inevitable change that will come into your life, think about the spirit that Saint Paul must have had, about his persistence as well as his upholding of love as the chief virtue, and do likewise.

We talked about *presence* in the first chapter when we discussed Brother Lawrence's classic book *The Practice of the Presence of God.* Let's look at this from a slightly different angle. Thomas Merton, in a discussion he conducted with a group of nuns toward the end of his life, talked about the presence of a speaker. He said that though some in the audience may have read his books, they still didn't really know him. "Presence is what counts," he said.[4]

I have pondered this statement many times since I read it a few years ago. As someone who is interested in education, I often think about the various means by which people learn. There is the written word, of course, as well as the spoken word. In our time, even more than in Merton's, there is the greater availability of using videotapes and other means of education. The Internet, for example, presents several new opportunities for learning.

But what about presence? If you really want to learn something, the best means is really to *experience* the teacher. Imagine how much more I would be able to learn from Merton if he were really here, in front of me. Then I could engage in a dialogue with him, could truly learn from him, in an open exchange.

Presence is what counts. We have the opportunity to experience this presence in our daily lives through centering our hearts upon Christ. We do this by simply acknowledging his presence, living with him, and expressing our faith for him. This living presence is really what counts.

One cannot live with Christ without exalting him. *Exaltation* means to praise and to glorify. Remembering Piper's view of Christian hedonism, we see that such praise is really our joy. It is our joy to praise Christ and to center ourselves upon him through this praise.

Exaltation is the chief means of centering our hearts upon Christ. One of the most powerful times of exaltation is through formal devotion. A practice of centering yourself on Christ, whether it be through daily study of the Scriptures or through set times of pausing to give praise, is essential to a changed-heart experience. Although I agree with Brother Lawrence that moving toward experiencing God as a constant presence is certainly beneficial, it is also important—as I am sure he, as a monk, would agree—to have set times for worship. Such times stop us from getting caught up in the daily toil of our lives and ensure that we will open our hearts to Christ at least at some point during the day. In my own experience, such spiritual pauses are vital. I have found it especially useful to plan five or six times during the day to stop and give praise. Sometimes this stopping is a pause, only lasting a moment or two. Still, this pause makes all the difference.

Using such methods as those found in this AGAPE acronym enables us to open our hearts to Christ and to live accordingly. Whatever method is used, it is essential to stay focused and to live within Christ (as he lives within you) during good times and bad. Only in doing this can we find the peace of the eternal presence that is our joy as Christians. Only through recognizing the Christ in our hearts, and seeing and bringing out the Christ in others, can we begin to experience the "love-feast" of life.

In writing this book, I have often thought about the acquaintance I mentioned at the beginning, the man consumed with hatred toward his unfaithful wife. As I said then, such are the real situations of this life. For those of us who are particularly sensitive, as I suspect my friend is, the difficulties of life can be extremely troubling, if not devastating. There is within these troubles, however, the hidden ground of love (to quote the title of a book of letters written by Thomas Merton). I believe that this ground is not really hidden and is not out there. Looking around for it in another person (as so many popular songs and movies would have us do) is not going to get us very far. Love is within each one of us, waiting to be discovered. I pray that you and I, as well as my friend, find this love, water it, and feel its growing presence in our lives.

The Journey: Now

The Journey to Christ begins and ends in the now. Consider the now—we have little else but this. It is only in the now that we experience. We may remember the past, or anticipate the future, but we do so only in the now.

As we conclude this book, think about your current experience. We have certainly implied that a Christ-centered heart is something like a journey. Still, it is best to recognize Christ now and experience the deep joy in your heart. Consider Jesus' own words in Luke when he says that the kingdom of God "is not coming with things that can be observed; nor will they say, 'Look, here it is!' or 'There it is!' For, in fact, the kingdom of God is among you" (17:20–21).

Notes

Notes to Chapter 1

1. Richard Carlson, *You Can Feel Good Again* (New York: Penguin Books, 1994), 82.
2. Henri J. M. Nouwen in Brother Lawrence of the Resurrection, *The Practice of the Presence of God* (New York: Doubleday, 1996), xi.
3. Ibid., 13.
4. Ibid., 21.
5. Ibid., 79–83.
6. Ibid., 96.

Notes to Chapter 2

1. Daniel Goleman, *Emotional Intelligence* (New York: Bantam Books, 1995), 170.
2. Bruno Cortis, M.D., *Heart and Soul: A Psychological and Spiritual Guide to Preventing and Healing Heart Disease* (New York: Villard Books, 1995), 93.
3. Goleman, 59.
4. Diogenes Allen, *The Path of Perfect Love* (Boston: Cowley Publications, 1992), 21–22.

Notes to Chapter 3

1. Diogenes Allen, *The Path of Perfect Love* (Boston: Cowley Publications, 1992), 66–67.

2. Richard Carlson, *You Can Be Happy No Matter What* (Novato, Calif.: New World Library, 1997), 53.
3. Ibid., 53.
4. Ibid., 6.
5. Ibid., 13.
6. Ibid., 56.
7. Carlson's "Principle of Separate Realities" is discussed on pp. 39–47 of *You Can Be Happy No Matter What*.
8. As discussed on pp. 59–69 of Carlson's *You Can Be Happy No Matter What*.
9. See Martin E. P. Seligman, *Learned Optimism* (New York: Alfred A. Knopf, 1991) for equally useful means of dealing with life's stresses and depression.

Notes to Chapter 5

1. Thomas Merton, *The Asian Journal of Thomas Merton* (New York: New Directions, 1968), 233–34, 235.
2. See also Henri Nouwen's account of his heart-changing experience as the result of a near-fatal accident in Henri J. M. Nouwen, *The Path of Freedom* (New York: Crossroad Publishing Company, 1995).
3. My understanding of the solitary experience and spiritual growth is gleaned from my personal experience with solitude, as well as the autobiographical works of Thomas Merton. See, for example, Merton's recent multivolume personal journals published by HarperSanFrancisco.

Notes to Chapter 6

1. David Nicholl, *Holiness* (New York: The Seabury Press, 1983), 154.
2. Diogenes Allen, *The Path of Perfect Love* (Boston: Cowley Publications, 1992), 2.
3. Ibid., 65.
4. Nicholl, *Holiness*, 37.
5. Ibid.

Notes to Chapter 7

1. I have altered the text slightly from the traditional version, changing the pronoun from plural (*we* and *us*) to first person singular (*I* and *me*) to give it a more personal feel.

2. Albert O. Hirschman, *Exit, Voice, and Loyalty* (Boston: Harvard University Press, 1972).

Notes to Chapter 8

1. The following statements from Nilus are found within Benedicta Ward, trans., *The Sayings of the Desert Fathers* (Kalamazoo, Mich.: Cistercian Publications, 1975), 153–54.
2. Larry Dossey, *Healing Words: The Power of Prayer and the Practice of Medicine* (San Francisco: HarperSanFrancisco, 1995).
3. Kathleen Norris, *The Cloister Walk* (New York: Riverhead Books, 1996), 46.
4. Mihaly Csikszentmihalyi, *Finding Flow: The Psychology of Engagement with Everyday Life* (New York: Basic Books, 1997), 89.

Notes to Chapter 9

1. David Nicholl, *Holiness* (New York: The Seabury Press, 1983), 145–46.
2. Thomas Merton, *The Silent Life* (New York: The Noonday Press, 1956), vii.
3. Ibid.
4. G. R. D. McLean, comp., *Praying with the Celts* (Grand Rapids, Mich.: Wm. B. Eerdmans Publishing Co., 1996), 77.
5. Esther de Waal, *The Celtic Way of Prayer* (New York: Doubleday, 1997), 70.
6. Mihaly Csikszentmihalyi, *Finding Flow* (New York: Basic Books, 1997), 29.

Notes to Chapter 10

1. John Piper, *Desiring God: Meditations of a Christian Hedonist* (Portland, Oreg.: Multnomah Press, 1986), 13<-14.
2. Ibid., 19.
3. Gillian Feeley-Harnik in Bruce M. Metzger and Michael D. Coogan, *The Oxford Companion to the Bible* (New York: Oxford University Press, 1993), 469.
4. Thomas Merton, *The Springs of Contemplation: A Retreat at the Abbey of Gethsemani* (New York: Farrar, Straus, & Giroux, 1992), 3.

About the Author

Rick Mathis manages medical policy research for Blue Cross Blue Shield of Tennessee. He received a Ph.D. in political science from the Johns Hopkins University and has taught courses at Loyola College in Baltimore and at the University of Tennessee in Chattanooga. He lectures and writes on topics as varied as Thomas Merton, healthcare, and ethics and politics. A lifelong student of philosophy and Christian spirituality, he likes to focus on the application of spirituality to everyday life. He lives in Soddy-Daisy, Tennessee, with his wife, Karen. They have two children.